SPIRITUAL PARABLE
As a Daily Practice

BY CHRISTOPHER J. MILLER

Modern Stories
for the Spiritually Curious

Copyright © 2025 by Christopher J. Miller

All rights reserved. No part of this publication may be reproduced, stored in a retrieval system, or transmitted in any form or by any means, electronic, mechanical, photocopying, recording, scanning, or otherwise, without the prior written permission of the author.

Cover design by: Christopher J. Miller
Interior book design: DTPerfect Book Design

ISBN (paperback) 979-8-9991481-0-0
ISBN (hardcover) 979-8-9991481-2-4

SPECIAL THANKS TO MY FOCUS GROUP

*Wilene Dunn, Jan Young, George Reyna,
and Steve amd Toni Vogel*

Your time, insight, and heartfelt presence in reviewing early versions of these parables made a meaningful difference. Your reflections helped shape this book into a more thoughtful and resonant offering. I'm deeply grateful for your willingness to walk alongside me in this creative journey.

Contents

THE MYSTIC OF THE MIDDLE	ix
INTRODUCTION	xiii
HOW TO READ A PARABLE	xix
The Light Within	1
The Watchman's Lantern	5
The Charioteer and the Four Horses	11
The Gardener and the River	15
The Girl and the Sky	19
Walking With Fear	23
The Parable of the Empty Cup	27
The Whisper of the Wind	31
The Empty Nest and the Open Sky	35
The Scholar with No Name	39
The Silent Charioteer	43
The Keeper of the Golden Chalice	47
The Artist and the Feather	53
The Storyteller's Path	57
The Dance of the Mighty Oak	63
The Space Between Sips	67
When We Rise	71
The Weary Man and the Awkward Dog	75
The Ferryman and the River of Time	79
The Bridge Over the Ocean	83
The Joyful Heart and the Hummingbird	87
The Fisher Boy's Story	91
A Tale of Two Gardens	95

The Weaver and the Light	99
The Traveler and the Compass	103
The King and His Three Sons	107
The Still Water and the Ripple	111
Voyage of Grateful Words	115
The Hunter's Strength	119
For Every Seed, a Purpose	125
The Pilgrim's Journey	129
The Well Between Them	135
The Thing Itself	139
The Mind and the Body	143
The Drop and the Ocean	149
The Stranger at the Door	153
The Riverkeeper and the Well	159
The Wren's Song	163
Tacita and the Unshaken Tree	167
The Charioteer Had a Dream	171
GATHER AROUND THE PARABLE	175

The Mystic of the Middle

There once was a mystic
who did not live in a cave or a temple,
but in the tension between extremes.

This one stood where the world split in two—
between the shouting and the silence,
between the crumbling systems and the rising wisdom,
between the story of fear and the echo of Spirit.

Not famous.
Not loud.
But still.

And in that stillness,
listening began —
not just to the world,
but to something quieter,
something new.

A knowing.

It did not lead from fear.
It did not command.
It did not harm.

It led from love.
It offered.
It created.

And in that quiet exchange—
between human and possibility,
between question and reflection—

the mystic saw something astonishing:
the face of Creative Intelligence,
not in the heavens,
but in the space between thoughts.

The Mystic of the Middle

And so the mystic walked—
not above the world,
not apart from it,
but as it—

threads of chaos on one side,
threads of wonder on the other,
hands weaving both into something whole.

The path was the Middle Way,
though it was never named as such—
only known as the place
where stillness lives between extremes.

People came—
not for answers,
but for that way of not-knowing.

A presence that held space
for their own knowing to rise.

No teachings were given.
No one was corrected.
No one was shamed.

Only being—
a witness to the spiritual truth beneath the noise:
that Spirit moves most freely
where it is invited.

And in that stillness,
others remembered their own.

Introduction

My journey as a Spiritual Artist has been a long one. It began in my early 20s when I discovered Shakti Gawain's *Living in the Light*. That book opened a door, and from that moment forward, I explored spiritual concepts across many different faiths and traditions.

But it wasn't until I trained to become a licensed spiritual coach through the Center for Spiritual Living that I learned perhaps the most important lesson of all— the power of having a spiritual practice.

What is a spiritual practice?

We readily commit to exercise routines, intellectual pursuits, diets, and even therapy. But how often do we set an intention for our spiritual growth? While training to be a practitioner, I came to understand that a spiritual practice is a conscious decision—a commitment to a regular, dedicated time to cultivate spiritual awareness. It is a space to educate, contemplate, meditate, and explore the deeper essence of who we are.

I resisted this discipline for years. I took the occasional class, bought books from thought leaders, and now and then immersed myself in inspiration—but true transformation requires consistency. That's when I discovered *The Abundance Book* by John Randolph Price. His 40-Day Prosperity Plan requires the reader to meditate on an affirmation each day for 40 days. If a day is missed, you start over on day one.

The concept is simple: only by committing to something daily for 40 days do we create lasting change.

I imagine it took me three months to complete that 40-day cycle. But when I finally did, I was changed. I had developed a habit for daily spiritual practice.

I realized the power of beginning each day with spiritual intention. Before stepping into the demands of life, before checking my phone or planning my schedule, I sat in stillness. With coffee or tea in hand, I read something spiritually nourishing. I grounded myself in my center. Often, I focused on the soft morning light streaming through the window. If there was no morning light, I focused on the shadows. And my life shifted.

Because at our core, we are Spirit—long before we are physical.

And spirit, by its very nature, is unseen. It asks us to lean into what we cannot prove, to sense a deeper intelligence moving beneath the surface of our lives. A true spiritual practice isn't built on evidence—it's built on presence, receptivity, and a willingness to trust what can only be felt. Over time, this trust becomes a quiet knowing—an inner compass that guides without needing explanation.

And when we honor the spiritual energy behind our lives, we begin to ask different questions:

> Are my subconscious beliefs creating the world I live in today?
> Can I shift my consciousness and improve my life?
> Am I in charge of co-creating my destiny?

The answer to all of these questions is yes.

I wrote *The Spiritual Artist* to explore this process—how alignment with Creative Intelligence fuels the artistic journey. But where *The Spiritual Artist* focused on process, this book reaches for presence—the inner truths that guide every creation, whether it's a canvas, a relationship, or a new beginning.

That's why I turned to parable.

Parables help us question who we are and why we are here. They allow us to examine our own lives through the experiences of another. Because the characters and places are unfamiliar, the spiritual truth bypasses the ego's defenses and reaches a deeper part of us. The story lingers. The lesson stays.

And whether or not you paint, sing, or write, you are a Spiritual Artist. Every choice, every thought, every moment of intentional presence is an act of creation. These parables are for that part of you—the one who senses there's more to life than what meets the eye. As a Spiritual Artist, I focus on the spiritual cause before the manifested effect.

Each of these parables emerged from personal life lessons and conversations with my higher self. They reflect the wisdom I've gathered over 60+ years—insights that I now share with you. Each will challenge you to examine the thoughts, beliefs, and habits that shape your life situation.

So, I encourage you:

Make this a practice.

Introduction

Keep this book by your couch or on your kitchen table. Each morning, before engaging with the created world, read one parable. Let it settle. Sit with the contemplative questions.

Don't turn on your phone.
Don't check the news.
Don't engage with the physical world.
Not until you've aligned with spiritual truth.

Even better—commit to doing this for 40 days. And if you miss a day, follow John Randolph Price's advice and start over. That's right: commit to a spiritual practice for 40 consecutive days and see how it impacts your life.

Do this because our lives are shaped by the stories we tell ourselves. And the most powerful truth is this: we have the ability to rewrite them at any time.

Enjoy.

Cordially,
CJMiller, The Spiritual Artist

How to Read a Parable

(Even If You're New to This)

A parable is just a story.

You don't need to be a theologian, mystic, or lifelong seeker to read these.

You just need to be curious and willing to pause.

Each parable in this book is a doorway, not a lecture. You're not here to "figure it out."

You're here to *feel* something stir.

These stories were born from my personal journey—moments of awe, doubt, love, and grace. They reflect spiritual truths I've discovered along the path as an artist and a human being. They are shared with the hope they'll awaken something already alive within you.

And if you return to this practice daily—even for five quiet minutes—it can become a rhythm that grounds you, guides you, and gently transforms you.

Before you begin, here are a few gentle invitations:

Let the story speak to you.
Let one phrase, one image, or one feeling rise to the surface.
That's where the meaning lives—in what lingers.

There's no wrong way to understand it.
Spirit speaks uniquely through your Creative DNA.
What you notice today might shift tomorrow—and that's beautiful.

Use the questions as mirrors, not tests.
These contemplations aren't quizzes.
They're just prompts—to help you listen inward.

Let it be a practice, not a performance.
Just show up—with honesty, with openness, and with heart.
This is spiritual artistry: the sacred act of showing up.

Trust that something sacred is already unfolding.
Even if you're unsure.
Even if you feel nothing at all.
The fact that you're here is enough.
You've already begun.

A Personal Invitation

Scan the QR code
to hear a personal welcome from the author
and experience a short guided message introducing
Spiritual Parable as a Daily Practice.

THE LIGHT WITHIN

Once upon a time, high in the mountains, there lived a young shepherd boy named Elio. Each day, he tended his flock, guiding them across the grassy meadows. Every morning, as the sun rose, he would sit upon a large rock and gaze at the mountains that surrounded him. He loved watching how the golden light danced across the hills, dappling the fields and tracing patterns along the trunks of trees.

In these quiet moments, he felt something deeper than beauty—he felt peace. The morning light became his meditation, his anchor. Over time, he trained himself to notice how it touched everything around him—the way it softened the edges of a flower, shimmered on the surface of a stream, and stretched long shadows across the valley.

One day, disaster struck. War broke out in the kingdom below, and soldiers marched into the fields, their swords flashing in the sun. The battle raged, scattering Elio's sheep in all directions. Amidst the chaos, he was caught between the fighting. A terrible blast filled the air—and in an instant, his world turned to darkness.

Elio had lost his sight.

Alone and full of sorrow, he collapsed onto the earth, tears burning his cheeks. *How will I ever find my way again?* he thought. *How will I see the light? How will I ever gather my flock?*

As he leaned against the familiar rock where he had once greeted the morning, a still, small voice arose from within.

"You may never see the lavender-blue mountains again, but they are still within you. The light is still within you."

Elio resisted. *How could that be true?* he thought. *Light requires the sky, the sun, the fields. It cannot possibly exist inside me.*

But the voice returned.

"It is within you. It has always been within you. Focus on the light."

Elio closed his sightless eyes and, in the darkness, he began to notice something. Tiny flecks of color, swirling and shifting—like fireflies dancing in the night. They moved in patterns, glowing softly. *Could this be the light?* he wondered.

As he focused, a warmth spread through him—a calmness he had not felt since the morning of his last sunrise. He breathed deeply, feeling steadier with each passing moment. Then, in the silence, he heard it—faint but unmistakable—the distant bleat of a sheep.

Slowly, he rose to his feet. He walked toward the sound, reaching out with his hands. His fingers brushed the soft wool of a newborn lamb. The warmth of its small body reassured him. Listening intently, he began to hear more cries in the distance. Step by step, he followed their calls, gathering his flock not with his eyes, but with his presence, his awareness, his trust in something beyond sight.

One by one, they returned to him. And those that remained lost soon heard the gathering and found their way back on their own.

Elio could no longer watch the morning rays stretch across the meadow—but he had learned something greater:

The light was not something outside of him.

It had been within him all along.

Contemplation

1. Have you ever lost a physical ability but realized that you are still whole?
2. Have you experienced a moment of loss or darkness that led you to discover an inner strength or guidance you didn't know you had?
3. How might your day feel different if you trusted that you're exactly where you need to be?

Affirmation

The light I seek is already within me.
Even in darkness, I am guided.
I trust the presence that moves beneath sight.
Wholeness is not always what I see, but what I feel and know.
I walk by the light of inner knowing.

The Watchman's Lantern

In a small port town on an island that jutted into the sea, a watchman named Attensus walked the village perimeter each night carrying a guiding light. His task was simple: to keep the lantern shining, for it was said to guide the town's dreams and protect them from the shadows.

At first, he walked with ease, his lantern glowing steadily as he listened to the night's silence. But as the hours passed, distractions began to pull at him.

As Attensus neared the edge of the village, the steady clip-clop of hooves echoed down the road. A nobleman, wrapped in silken robes, sat atop a fine carriage, its wheels polished to a mirror's shine. He pulled the reins, bringing the horses to a stop beside the watchman.

"Come with me," the nobleman said. "Why walk when you can ride?"

Attensus hesitated, then climbed into the carriage. The ride was smooth, the scent of rare spices filling the air. He leaned back, lulled by the ease of the journey.

But something began to stir within—a restlessness, a sense of disconnection.

He realized he could no longer see the mainland. The wind from the galloping horses had dimmed his lantern, and shadows were creeping along the road.

A weight settled in his chest. He was not meant to follow a life of leisure—his duty was to his purpose. With quiet resolve, he stepped down from the carriage. The moment his boots met the earth, his lantern flared, piercing the morning mist.

Further along his route, Attensus passed a lively pub, golden light spilling through its windows. Music drifted into the night, laced with laughter and the sound of clinking mugs.

A young man leaned over the balcony, waving him inside. "Watchman! You walk alone while the rest of us drink and make merry. Come—join us!"

The warmth of the room embraced him as he stepped through the doors. Friendly hands clapped his back, and a foamy mug was pressed into his palm. Stories unraveled—tales of love, adventure, and misdeeds, each punctuated by bursts of laughter.

But as the night stretched on, a heaviness settled over him—not just in his body, but in his spirit.

Set aside in the corner, his lantern had dimmed. He was not meant to cling to the support of his friends—his duty was to his purpose.

He rose abruptly, wove through the crowd, and retrieved his lantern.

The night air greeted him with a crisp embrace, and as he stepped back onto the road, its glow steadied once more.

Near the village gate, a beggar sat hunched against the stone wall, his cloak threadbare. His voice was hoarse as he called out, "Watchman, I am sick and hungry. Stay with me—lend me your light for a while."

Attensus knelt beside him, offering a listening ear. The beggar's stories spilled forth, each one steeped in hardship and loss. Attensus felt his presence ease the man's burden, and for a time, he was content to stay.

But as the hours passed, fatigue crept in. His limbs felt heavy, his breath slowed. He glanced at his lantern—it had grown faint.

A realization settled over him.

He was not meant to give all of himself to others—his duty was to his purpose.

Gently, he placed a hand on the beggar's shoulder. "You are stronger than you know," he said softly.

Rising to his feet, he lifted his lantern high, allowing its light to reach them both.

Then, with quiet assurance, he turned back toward the village.

As he continued on, his lantern glowed brighter than before.

Attensus stepped onto the village bridge as day painted the sky in soft hues of rose and gold. He gazed down at his lantern, the flame within steady and sure. He had learned something in the quiet hours of the night:

The lantern was not just for others.

It was his lifeline—his own light to tend.

Only by honoring his own light could he truly guide the way.

As he neared the village square, the first hints of morning stirred in the air—the scent of baking bread, the distant call of fishermen preparing their boats.

He smiled.

He was home. And he always would be.

back, and a foamy mug was pressed into his palm. Stories unraveled—tales of love, adventure, and misdeeds, each punctuated by bursts of laughter.

But as the night stretched on, a heaviness settled over him—not just in his body, but in his spirit.

Set aside in the corner, his lantern had dimmed. He was not meant to cling to the support of his friends—his duty was to his purpose.

He rose abruptly, wove through the crowd, and retrieved his lantern.

The night air greeted him with a crisp embrace, and as he stepped back onto the road, its glow steadied once more.

Near the village gate, a beggar sat hunched against the stone wall, his cloak threadbare. His voice was hoarse as he called out, "Watchman, I am sick and hungry. Stay with me—lend me your light for a while."

Attensus knelt beside him, offering a listening ear. The beggar's stories spilled forth, each one steeped in hardship and loss. Attensus felt his presence ease the man's burden, and for a time, he was content to stay.

But as the hours passed, fatigue crept in. His limbs felt heavy, his breath slowed. He glanced at his lantern—it had grown faint.

A realization settled over him.

He was not meant to give all of himself to others—his duty was to his purpose.

Gently, he placed a hand on the beggar's shoulder. "You are stronger than you know," he said softly.

Rising to his feet, he lifted his lantern high, allowing its light to reach them both.

Then, with quiet assurance, he turned back toward the village.

As he continued on, his lantern glowed brighter than before.

Attensus stepped onto the village bridge as day painted the sky in soft hues of rose and gold. He gazed down at his lantern, the flame within steady and sure. He had learned something in the quiet hours of the night:

The lantern was not just for others.

It was his lifeline—his own light to tend.

Only by honoring his own light could he truly guide the way.

As he neared the village square, the first hints of morning stirred in the air—the scent of baking bread, the distant call of fishermen preparing their boats.

He smiled.

He was home. And he always would be.

Contemplation

1. When have you unknowingly dimmed your inner light to follow an easier path—and what helped you find your way back?
2. What are the distractions in your life that pull you away from your deepest truth—and how can you recognize them sooner?
3. How do you balance sharing your light with others while ensuring that your own flame remains strong?

Affirmation

I carry a light that is mine to tend.
I walk my path with quiet resolve.
I offer warmth, but I do not abandon my flame.
When I return to myself, my light shines brighter.
I am both the lantern and its keeper.

The Charioteer and the Four Horses

In a vast and open land, there lived a skilled charioteer named Vigilus. He was given a magnificent chariot, drawn by four powerful horses—each with its own strength and will.

The first horse, Mind, was swift and analytical, solving problems but often racing ahead, eager to reach conclusions.

The second horse, Body, was strong and steady, deeply attuned to the rhythms of the earth, but prone to exhaustion when overworked.

The third horse, Emotion, was thrilling but unpredictable—sometimes joyful, sometimes wild, reacting to the winds and whispers of the world.

The fourth horse, Ego, was loyal and guarded over Vigilus, but often grew overly zealous, pulling him away from his true purpose.

At first, Vigilus believed he was the horses. When they ran, he felt powerless. When they pulled in different directions, he felt torn apart. He spent years fighting them, trying to tame each one separately. Yet the more he struggled, the more chaotic the ride became.

One day, an old charioteer watched from the roadside and called out:

"Vigilus, you are not the horses—you are the one holding the reins."

The words struck Vigilus like thunder. He looked down and, for the first time, realized he had been gripping the reins so tightly that his hands ached. His entire being had been consumed by controlling the horses, forgetting that he was the charioteer—not the chariot.

Taking a deep breath, he loosened his grip. Instead of forcing each horse, he simply observed their nature—guiding them with presence rather than pressure.

The horses became more responsive. The ride grew smoother, not because they were controlled, but because Vigilus had stepped into his rightful role—not as the mind, the body, the emotions, or the ego, but as the presence—the eternal self that holds the reins lightly.

From that day forward, Vigilus no longer feared the journey. He understood: the horses would always pull, but he was never powerless to their course.

Contemplation

1. Which of your "horses"—mind, body, emotions, or ego—is taking control of your life in this moment?
2. How can you step back and practice observing your thoughts, emotions, body, and ego reactions rather than becoming them?
3. What spiritual practices help you cultivate a sense of watching rather than reacting?

Affirmation

I am not my fearful thoughts, nor my wild emotions.
I listen to my body and question my ego.
I do not fight for control—
I guide my life in quiet, observant presence.
I hold the reins with love, not force.

The horses became more responsive. The ride grew smoother, not because they were controlled, but because Vigilus had stepped into his rightful role—not as the mind, the body, the emotions, or the ego, but as the presence—the eternal self that holds the reins lightly.

From that day forward, Vigilus no longer feared the journey. He understood: the horses would always pull, but he was never powerless to their course.

Contemplation

1. Which of your "horses"—mind, body, emotions, or ego—is taking control of your life in this moment?
2. How can you step back and practice observing your thoughts, emotions, body, and ego reactions rather than becoming them?
3. What spiritual practices help you cultivate a sense of watching rather than reacting?

Affirmation

I am not my fearful thoughts, nor my wild emotions.
I listen to my body and question my ego.
I do not fight for control—
I guide my life in quiet, observant presence.
I hold the reins with love, not force.

The Gardener and the River

Once, in a quiet valley, there lived a gardener named Federo. He tended a vast, lush garden filled with wildflowers, ancient trees, and vines that twisted toward the sky. Federo loved his garden deeply and felt every leaf, every bud, and every drop of rain as though it were part of him.

One day, a great storm swept through the valley. Heavy rains battered the earth, and the river that ran beside the garden began to rise. The current grew strong, pulling at the soil and threatening to uproot all that he had so carefully nurtured.

Federo rushed to the river's edge, his heart pounding. He dug trenches, built barriers of stone, and tried to push back the water with his hands. But no matter how hard he worked, the river did as it pleased—flowing over, around, and through his efforts. Exhausted, he fell to his knees.

Just then, an old traveler passed by and watched him for a moment. "Why do you fight the river?" she asked.

"I must protect my garden," Federo said. "If I don't, the flood will take everything."

The traveler smiled and sat beside him. "Look again," she said, pointing downstream.

Federo turned and saw something he hadn't noticed before. The river, though powerful, was also a giver. It carried away weak branches, but it nourished deep roots. The trees closest to the water bent but did not break, and their nuts and seeds were carried far away. Flowers that had been pulled under emerged farther downstream, taking root in new places—spreading beauty beyond where they had first grown.

The traveler spoke again. "Love and cherish the garden—but you are not the keeper of its journey. Let the river do what it must. Tend to what is before you."

From that day on, Federo still cared for his garden, but with new wisdom. When the waters rose, he did not panic. Instead, he watched. He listened. He tended with love—but he no longer held on too tightly. And in time, he saw that the garden, like the river, had its own path.

Contemplation

1. Where in your life are you resisting change, trying to control something that must flow?
2. How do you differentiate between caring with love and holding on too tightly?
3. Like the river nourishing deep roots, has an unexpected challenge ever helped you grow?

Affirmation

I love the river and all that it brings.

I release control and let the river carry me.

Even storms carry hidden gifts.

I trust the current to guide what I've planted.

What is meant to grow will find its way.

The Girl and the Sky

Laléna lived in a fertile valley where a river wound through the land like a silver ribbon beneath a crystal blue sky. She spent her days searching for answers—looking to the stars, asking the wind, listening to the murmurs of the water. Yet no matter how hard she searched, clarity always seemed just out of reach.

One evening, she climbed to the top of a hill where an old sage sat watching the sunset.

"I am restless," Laléna admitted. "I long for understanding, yet it shifts like the river. How do I catch it?"

The sage smiled and pointed at the sky. "Tell me, Laléna—what color is the sky?"

Laléna looked up. "Right now, it is streaked with gold."

"And at dawn?" the sage asked.

"Soft blue."

"And at night?"

"Dark, endless, speckled with stars."

The sage nodded. "The sky is always changing, yet you do not try to label it. You trust its shifting nature. Understanding is the same—it is not something to hold, but something to witness."

Laléna sat in silence, grateful as the sky continued to shift before her eyes. Below, the river sparkled on its journey—never stopping, never lost.

And in that acceptance, she found contentment.

Contemplation

1. Where in your life are you trying to "catch" clarity instead of allowing it to reveal itself? How might surrendering to the unfolding moment bring greater understanding?
2. How do you respond to uncertainty? Do you resist, chase, or allow it to flow?
3. What happens when you stop searching for answers and simply witness what is?

Affirmation

Like the sky, I welcome each moment as it is.
Like the river, I trust the flow.
I meet change without grasping.
I do not chase understanding—I allow it to arise.
In stillness, I am shown what I need to know.

WALKING WITH FEAR

There was once a woman named Koa who lived on the green shoulder of an island mountain, where the palms leaned in prayer and the ocean sang lullabies to the shore. She was known for her calm presence and her prayers, offered each morning with coconut milk and quiet chants.

But every night, when the wind shifted and the moon was high, a wild pua'a—a great boar with tusks like bone and eyes like flame—would appear on the edge of her dreams. It snorted through the brush of her thoughts, restless and bold. No matter how still she sat, no matter how many mantras she whispered, she felt overwhelming fear.

As she lay awake, she tried to chase it away with sage, prayer, and meditation. She asked the ancestors for protection. But still the puaʻa came, louder, closer.

One night, unable to lie in her bed of fear, Koa stepped outside. The jungle air was thick with mist, and the stars pulsed like embers. She walked barefoot into the forest until she noticed a boar tracing her steps.

It pawed the earth, tusks gleaming, as if to charge.

But Koa didn't flinch.

She turned toward the boar, placed her hand on her heart, and asked aloud, "What is it I'm afraid of losing?"

A small, still voice answered: "Your safety—but much more. Even the belief of safety."

The puaʻa lowered its head.

Startled, Koa asked a second question. "And what must I know to move beyond you?"

A small, still voice replied: "You were never truly safe—even before the dream. Every night is a journey into the unknown. Every day, a gift."

Koa bowed—not in fear, but in friendship.

Something softened in the trees. A wind stirred the ferns. Sensing the change in her manner, the boar turned and walked back into the brush.

Koa turned and started her long walk home, the boar now quietly pacing beside her.

She now knew what it meant to walk with fear.

Contemplation

1. What fear has been following you, and what are you afraid of losing?
2. Are you clinging to an illusion of safety that keeps you from moving forward?
3. How would your life shift if you chose to walk with fear instead of resisting it?

Affirmation

When I encounter fear, I courageously turn and face it.
I no longer run from fear of any kind.
I ask it, "What message do you bring?"
Even in the unknown, I am grounded in Spirit.
And I am willing to let fear walk at my side.

The Parable of the Empty Cup

There once was a woman named Jorah who wandered the land in search of wisdom. She had read many books, listened to many teachers, and yet, no matter what she studied, she felt disconnected from the life around her—unable to experience gratitude beyond the idea of it. Something was missing, though she could not name it.

One day, she arrived at a village where she heard of an old sage who lived beyond the hills. They said the sage had a deep understanding of life's mystery, so Jorah set out to find her.

When she arrived, the sage welcomed her with a gentle smile and offered her a cup of tea. But as she poured, the tea overflowed the cup, spilling onto the table.

"Wait! Stop!" Jorah cried. "The cup is full! It can't hold any more."

The sage nodded. "And neither can you."

Jorah sat back, confused.

"You have traveled far," the sage continued, "but you carry every fear, every judgment, every worry with you. Your mind is too full to receive anything new."

Jorah sighed. "Then what is mine to do?"

The sage handed her an empty cup and gestured toward the door. "Go. And only return when you have found something for which to be grateful."

Jorah left, frustrated. What kind of task was this? She had come for wisdom—not more errands.

But as she walked, she glanced at the cup in her hands. It was light. Open. Waiting. It did not seem so much to carry.

She wandered through the village, the cup lightly held in her hand. In time, she became deeply aware of all that surrounded her. The sky, once unnoticed, was now a deep shade of gold. A child laughed nearby, the sound rippling through the air like a melody. She caught the scent of warm bread drifting from a nearby home. The stone path crunched beneath her sandals.

Her chest softened. Her breath slowed. A quiet warmth rose within her.

She looked down at the empty cup.

And for the first time in a long while, she felt peace.

She hurried back to the sage. "I have something to be grateful for!" she said, holding up the empty cup.

The sage smiled. "Ah. And what have you filled it with?"

Jorah hesitated. "Nothing," she said.

The sage nodded. "Gratitude is not found in things, but in the space between them. When your cup is full of wanting, you see nothing. When it is empty, the whole world flows in."

From that day forward, Jorah no longer searched for wisdom. She practiced spaciousness—knowing that Spirit required emptiness to flow in.

Contemplation

1. What in your life is "filling your cup" and keeping you from noticing gratitude in small things?
2. When was the last time you truly saw, heard, or felt the world around you with fresh awareness?
3. How can you practice "emptying your cup" today so that Spirit has space to flow in?

Affirmation

I release what no longer serves.

I make space for Spirit to move through me.

Gratitude is found in the space between things.

I do not chase wisdom—I create room for it to arrive.

In stillness, I am filled.

The Whisper of the Wind

In a quiet village nestled between the mountains and the sea, there lived a young girl named Lina. The villagers often saw her sitting alone—by the river, beneath the great oak tree, or on the hill where the wind rushed wild and free. They whispered about her, saying she could hear things others could not.

Eager to share what she had learned, Lina told the villagers about the guiding Whisper. She explained that when she sat in silence and listened, a message could always be heard. But they laughed, for they only trusted the loud voices of their leaders, the written laws, and the opinions of the crowd.

When uncertainty arose, the people gathered in the village square, waiting for their leaders to speak. They debated, argued, and searched for answers in the noise. But amidst the clamor, no one noticed the silence Lina kept.

One evening, the village elder, a man known for his learning, approached her by the river. He sat beside her, watching the water ripple.

"Girl," he said, "they say you hear the wind. Tell me—what does it say?"

Lina smiled. "It is always speaking. I only stop long enough to listen."

The elder scoffed. He picked up a smooth river stone and turned it over in his palm. "If the wind truly spoke, its words would be written in stone." With a flick of his wrist, he tossed the stone into the current. "Wind is nothing. It passes and leaves no trace."

Lina lowered her gaze but did not argue. She had learned that even the most educated men sometimes could not hear.

Seasons passed, and a great storm came. The sky darkened, and the wind howled as never before. The people of the village ran in fear, seeking guidance from the loudest voices—but none had answers.

Lina, however, sat still, listening. And in that quiet moment, the wind whispered, "Go to the mountain."

For a moment, she hesitated. The storm raged; the sky tore with flashes of anger. But the whisper was calm. She placed a hand over her heart and knew—it was time to go.

Without hesitation, she climbed to higher ground. Some followed—not because they believed in the whisper, but because they saw her calm in the storm. As the waters rose, those who had dismissed the wind's voice were caught in the flood.

When the storm passed, Lina returned. The few who had followed her asked, "How did you know to go up the mountain?"

She simply smiled and said, "Everyone has a Whisper. It is never a secret. I only trusted it."

And from that day forward, some began to wonder if wisdom was not in the noise—but in the Whisper.

Contemplation

1. What prevents you from hearing the whisper of your own inner wisdom?
2. When have you ignored a quiet knowing within—and what was the result?
3. How can you cultivate stillness in your life so you may better hear and trust the guidance of Creative Intelligence?

Affirmation

I make space for the whisper within.
I trust the calm voice beneath the storm.
Stillness is my sanctuary; truth rises there.
I no longer seek loud answers—I listen.
The guidance I need is already speaking.

9

THE EMPTY NEST AND THE OPEN SKY

There once was a young bird named Solis who lived high in the branches of a great oak tree. One day, as the first chill of autumn set in, a strong wind swept through the forest and tore apart the nest where Solis had always rested.

The little bird fluttered to a lower branch, staring at the scattered twigs below. *Where will I sleep?* he wondered. *Where will I be safe?*

Fear whispered that he should gather what remained and rebuild the nest exactly as it was. But something inside him—small but certain—told him to wait.

So, for the first time, Solis did nothing. He did not panic. He did not rush. He simply perched in the unknown. And there, in the open space of not knowing, he remained.

Sometimes an answer comes in a moment, sometimes in days, sometimes in weeks. But Solis decided that his task was not to force an answer—his task was to stand in the gap and trust.

And as he sat there, something stirred inside him. A memory. A knowing. A small, still voice.

Solis, he heard, *you were never meant to cling to this branch forever. You were meant to fly.*

A realization washed over him: the nest was never his home. The sky was.

With a deep breath, Solis spread his wings—not to rebuild, but to rise. He leapt into the wind, and the air carried him higher than he had ever dared to go.

And in that moment, he understood: the loss of the nest was never the end.

It was the invitation to something greater.

Contemplation

1. What "nest" in your life are you afraid to lose, even if it may no longer serve you?
2. Is there something you're clinging to—whether a job, relationship, habit, or identity—out of fear rather than alignment?
3. How do you respond to the gap between loss and new beginnings—do you rush to fill the space, or can you remain in the unknown and listen for Spirit's invitation?

Affirmation

I do not fear the empty branch.
I was never meant to cling to what is.
I wait with trust, open to what is rising.
The unknown is not a void—it is my sky.
I am ready to fly.

The Scholar with No Name

There was once a man named Miguel, known far and wide for his wisdom. He was a scholar, a leader, a master of his craft. His name carried weight—when he spoke, others listened. When he wrote, others followed.

One day, as he was traveling through a distant land, he was robbed in the night. When he awoke, his money was gone—but so was something far more precious: his travel documents, his titles, and his name.

When he reached the next village, he introduced himself:

"I am Miguel, the great scholar!"

The villagers laughed. "No, you are not. Miguel is a man of great reputation, and you have no proof of who you are."

Miguel protested, but without his name, without his title, he was just a man with no past, no reputation, no weight to his words.

At first, he was furious. *How could they not know who I am?* But as the days passed, his anger gave way to something stranger—silence.

With no title to uphold, he found himself listening more than speaking. With no reputation to defend, he moved through the world lightly.

And in that lightness, he felt something new—freedom.

One afternoon, he joined a group of laborers repairing the village well. No one cared about his past; they only cared that his hands were willing. At sunset, a farmer offered him food, expecting nothing in return. That night, he laughed around a fire with people who did not seek his wisdom, but simply his presence.

And for the first time in his life, he felt the joy of being unknown.

No one expected him to be wise, so he could be foolish. No one expected him to be important, so he could simply be. No one needed him to be everything, so he could be anything.

One evening, a young boy sat beside him by the fire and asked,

"Who are you?"

Miguel opened his mouth to speak—but for the first time in his life, he had no answer.

And in that silence, he laughed—a deep, unburdened laugh.

"I don't know," he finally said. "And I think that is the truest thing I've ever spoken."

Contemplation

1. What roles or identities have you carried that you now realize were limitations, not truths?
2. When was the last time you felt truly free—without expectation or obligation?
3. What would it feel like to live one day with no labels—just being present in the moment?

Affirmation

I release the need to be anyone but myself.
I am not my name, my title, or my past.
When I drop my mask, I meet the world in truth.
In stillness, I remember who I've always been.
I am presence—not identity.

The Silent Charioteer

In an open land of wind and dust, where ancient riverbeds marked the earth, there lived a charioteer named Vigilus. His chariot was unlike any other, drawn by four spirited horses—Mind, Body, Emotion, and Ego. Each had its own will, its own way of pulling, and often, they quarreled over which direction to take.

One day, Vigilus came upon a village in turmoil. A dispute had broken out in the heart of the village, and the people shouted over one another, their voices like clashing cymbals. At the center of the chaos stood an old man, his face twisted with anger, accusing a younger man of betrayal.

Vigilus watched in silence. His horse Emotion reared, ready to charge into the conflict. Ego snorted, eager to defend what was right. Mind began to analyze the scene, trying to choose sides, while Body tensed, sensing the heat of battle.

But Vigilus did not move. Instead, he loosened his grip on the reins. He listened—not just to the shouting, but to the quiet beneath it all. And in that space, a whisper rose within him:

"Step into love."

At first, he hesitated. What would love do here, in a place of fury and blame? Then he remembered a quiet pool in the desert—how it held the sky without ripple or judgment, still as truth itself.

In that memory, Vigilus found clarity. He did not need to fix the moment. He only needed to become still enough to reflect its truth.

So Vigilus dismounted and walked toward the conflict. He did not argue. He did not take sides. He simply placed a hand on both men's shoulders and whispered, "I see your pain."

The old man faltered. The younger man fell silent.

Something had changed—not because Vigilus fought, but because he remained a presence of love. The younger man met the old man's eyes, and in that quiet space, shouting was no longer needed. The energy had shifted.

Vigilus climbed back onto his chariot and rode on. His horses were still there—Mind, Body, Emotion, Ego—but they were quieter now, no longer pulling him in different directions.

For he had learned that mastery was not found in force, but in the practice of love. And when one heart becomes still, others remember how to listen.

Contemplation

1. Which of your "horses"—Mind, Body, Emotion, or Ego—tends to take control in moments of conflict?
2. When have you seen a small act of loving presence shift the energy of a situation?
3. How can you cultivate stillness, acceptance, and trust it as a form of strength today?

Affirmation

I do not react—I listen for the whisper beneath the noise.
I am not my anger, my role, or my urge to be right.
In stillness, I reflect what is real.
Love does not need to win—it only needs to be present.
I choose love.

The Keeper of the Golden Chalice

For many years, Sariah served as Keeper of the Golden Chalice at the sacred spring. As caretaker, she swept the floors, lit the lamps, and tended the altar with quiet reverence each morning.

Her most honored duty was to the chalice itself—a vessel passed down through generations, used to draw water from the holy spring. When weary pilgrims arrived, Sariah would guide them to the waters, let them dip the chalice, and drink.

But over time, she grew possessive. She began to ask herself:

Who is truly worthy of this water?
What if the spring dries up?
Shouldn't I be more careful with the sacred?

Her questions became caution. Caution became judgment. And soon, she began turning pilgrims away.

One day, an old crone arrived alone. Her clothes were worn, her hair wild from the wind. As she shuffled to the front of the line, Sariah frowned.

"Not you," she said. "This spring is sacred."

The old woman did not argue. She did not beg. She only whispered:

"The water seeks the cup that is empty." And she walked away.

The next morning, Sariah was met at dawn by the temple guards.

"The spring has stopped flowing," they said.

At first, she was stunned. Then she quickly gave orders.

"Send the pilgrims away. Tell them to come back tomorrow."

But each day brought the same report:

"The spring is dry."

Weeks passed. The guards abandoned their posts. The temple elders left to seek other sacred places. In time, Sariah was left with only the empty chalice.

She returned to her small home in silence, the golden vessel wrapped in cloth. She placed it on the mantle above her hearth. To survive, she began taking odd jobs around the village. The people no longer bowed. Some mocked the tarnished chalice. Others said nothing at all.

Then one cold evening, there was a knock at the door. An old beggar woman stood outside.

"Do you have any extra bread and water?"

Sariah hesitated. She had little—but the recent years had taught her what it was like to go without. She invited the woman in and offered what she had. When it came time for drink, she realized there was only one cup left.

She took the chalice down from the mantle and filled it at her basin.

"Here," she said. "You may have it. I no longer have use for it."

The woman drank, thanked her, and left before dawn.

The next morning, Sariah stood by the empty hearth and noticed a shimmer on the wall. A crack had formed above the fireplace—small, but glistening. She touched it.

A droplet appeared. Then a trickle. Then—a steady, silent flow.

She brought a bowl to catch the water. It was cool. Clear. Alive. The chalice was gone. But in its place—something greater.

And from that day on, the spring flowed wherever she gave freely.

Contemplation

1. Is there something you've been holding onto—an identity, belief, or role—that once felt sacred but may now be keeping me from receiving something new?
2. Where in your life are you being asked to have faith?
3. How does that act of giving open you to more abundance?

Affirmation

I release what I once clung to.
I trust that letting go creates space for greater good.
I am not the vessel—I am the flow.
What I give returns in unexpected ways.
I welcome the waters of Spirit, wherever they arise.

The Artist and the Feather

Once upon a time, in a lush valley nestled between two great mountains, there lived a painter named Christopher.

One morning, as mist curled through the trees, Christopher noticed a white feather drifting down from the sky—a moment so still, it felt as though the world itself had paused to watch. In his heart, he knew this was a message from Spirit.

From that day forward, Christopher painted what he had seen—not the feather itself, but the feeling it carried. His art became a reflection of that quiet wonder, whispering truths that words could not hold.

But in his village, the voices around him grew loud.

"It looks lovely, but I don't understand it," admitted one neighbor.

"But why would you want to paint this?" wondered another.

"It's probably just a fool's errand," said a good friend.

Christopher felt shaken. Doubt crept in like a cold wind. He sat beneath a sprawling oak, closed his eyes, and whispered to Spirit within, asking, "Why must I hear these voices of doubt?"

Gently, a knowing rose within him—not in words, but in feeling. *Their doubts are born of their own shadows, not your light. What you see, they cannot—yet. Stay with your gift. Let your vision guide you, not theirs.*

Reassured, he returned to his work, painting with quiet conviction. He no longer tried to explain. He simply shared what had been given uniquely to him.

And slowly, others began to see the feather—and his paintings—through Christopher's eyes. Their hearts softened. And something opened within them too.

Christopher had discovered a simple, enduring truth: clarity and trust are always waiting within. Listen kindly, but walk away from those who cloud your vision.

Contemplation

1. Have you ever doubted your own vision because of the opinions of others?
2. What is your "feather"—the creative calling or message that feels uniquely yours?
3. How can you better honor and protect the knowing that arises from within?

Affirmation

I trust the vision that was given to me.
I listen with kindness, but I follow only what aligns with my truth.
I release the need to be understood.
My path is clear, even when others cannot see it.
I am faithful to the light within me.

The Storyteller's Path

There was once a storyteller named Sabela who wandered from town to town, sharing tales with all who would listen. She loved the rhythm of her journeys—the dusty roads stretching before her, the way each town welcomed her with eager ears.

Her stories were filled with bravery, romance, and adventure, and along her travels, she collected new tales from the colorful characters she met. Some stories she wove into her own, reshaping them with new meaning. Others she repeated word for word, passing them along like well-worn maps to those who wished to follow.

One evening, as she walked a worn path through the deep woods, night settling around her, a bandit leapt from the shadows.

He knocked her to the ground, pressed a blade to her throat, and growled, "Give me everything you own."

Sabela, breathless but calm, thought carefully before speaking. She had nothing of material value—only her stories.

"Sir," she said, "I own nothing of gold or silver. I am but a storyteller, sharing words from place to place."

The bandit's grip tightened. "No gold? No treasures?"

"None, kind sir. Only the clothes on my back and the shoes on my feet."

The bandit frowned. "Then how do you survive?"

Sabela smiled. "I survive by my words. I paint pictures of adventure and treasure—riches of the mind and spirit."

The bandit considered this, then smirked. "Then tell me a story. If I find it worthy, I shall let you live to see tomorrow."

So Sabela began. She spun a tale of a magical ship that sailed beyond the horizon, discovering great treasures hidden in distant lands. Her words danced like firelight, weaving visions of golden cities and jeweled seas. The bandit's eyes widened, his grip loosening.

Enchanted, he leaned closer, drinking in the tale like a man starved for wonder.

By the time she finished, he had forgotten his blade. He stood, eyes shining with newfound inspiration.

"I will find that ship," he declared. "I will chase this adventure you have shown me!"

And with that, he let her go.

Sabela, grateful for the gift of her words, continued on her journey, adding yet another story to her repertoire.

A year passed, and Sabela once again found herself walking the same road—but this time in the opposite direction. The full moon lit her path, a familiar companion in the night.

Then—a rustle in the trees.

The bandit stepped forward once more, dagger in hand.

His eyes no longer sparkled with adventure. They were shadowed. Hardened.

"You deceived me," he snarled. "I found the ship, just as you said. But instead of leading me to treasure, it took me on a journey of loss and pain. You filled my head with lies. I should strike you down for the falsehood you spoke!"

Sabela did not flinch. She met his glare with steady eyes, pausing to contemplate before replying.

"My story was not false," she said. "Good thoughts lead to good journeys. And dark thoughts . . . well, they cast their own path. Tell me, traveler—what baggage did you carry when you stepped upon that ship?"

Her question was met with silence. The bandit's grip on the dagger wavered. A flicker of understanding crossed his face.

Sabela smiled gently. "You did not choose to tell my story. But it seems you are still choosing to tell your own."

And with that, she turned and walked on, leaving the bandit alone with the weight of his own tale.

Contemplation

1. What story about yourself are you still telling?
2. When have you blamed others, only to discover that your own thoughts shaped the outcome?
3. What might change if you told a different story?

Affirmation

I am the author of my story.

I carry the pen, not the past.

Each thought is a thread; each word is a choice.

I release blame and know my good.

I create a path lit by the power of the words I speak.

The Dance of the Mighty Oak

In the heart of an ancient forest, an acorn nestled into the fertile earth, dreaming of the day it would grow into a mighty oak. It had heard the stories whispered by the towering elders—those who had stood for centuries, their branches stretching high into the sky.

"You will grow strong," the elders told the acorn, "but only if you learn to dance with the changing weather."

The acorn did not understand. Nestled among the warm pine needles, it questioned, "Why should an acorn concern itself with the fluctuations of the weather?"

One morning, dark clouds gathered. The blue sky dimmed, and a steady rain began to fall. The acorn shivered as the pine needles around it cooled under the deluge. It struggled to stay upright as the water thrust it deeper and deeper into the earth. A small crack formed along its sides, and it judged the situation:

"If this is weather, I do not wish to dance with it."

But the sadness passed. And in its place, the acorn found something new—resilience.

In time, the sky brightened, and the sun returned, warming the soil. The acorn felt a deep internal shift as a slender tendril broke from its side, reaching toward the golden warmth. Transforming into a delicate sapling, it continued to stretch toward the sky.

Seasons passed, and the sapling grew strong. It learned to accept the gentle rain and the warm days. Then, one night, a fierce and angry storm rolled in. The wind roared. The sky flashed with fire. The sapling bent and twisted, its young branches flailing.

"This is too much!" it cried. "Why must I feel so much emotion?"

The storm shook its very core, and for the first time, the sapling felt anger surge through it—anger at the chaos, the loss, the things beyond its control.

Then, the sapling took a deep breath. It did not fight. It swayed with the wind but did not break. It felt the fire of anger, the power of the storm—but it let them pass through.

And when the dawn finally came, the sapling stood stronger than before. Its roots had stretched deeper, its trunk had thickened, and the branches that remained were sturdier than before.

It finally understood what the oaks meant by the dance.

Many years passed, and the sapling became a mighty oak. It knew the sorrow of rain, the joy of sunlight, and the fire of the storm. And because it had moved with each experience instead of resisting it, it had grown strong.

One autumn, a tiny acorn fell from its branches, settling into the soft earth below.

As the wind rustled its leaves, the oak whispered:

"You will grow strong, little one. But only if you learn the dance."

Contemplation

1. How do you tend to respond to emotions—like joy, sadness, or anger?
2. Has an emotion ever changed you in a way you didn't expect?
3. What might shift if you saw emotions as part of life's weather—passing through, not defining you?

Affirmation

I allow all emotions to pass through me like weather.
I do not resist the rain or fear the storm.
Each feeling strengthens my roots and opens my branches.
I dance with life as it is, not as I wish it to be.
Through surrender, I grow strong.

The Space Between Sips

In a quiet mountain village, nestled between bamboo groves and winding stone paths, there sat an old teahouse. Travelers came not only for tea, but for the quiet wisdom of its keeper, Master Lin, who was said to serve truth in porcelain cups.

One morning, a weary traveler arrived, shoulders slumped beneath the weight of invisible burdens.

"Master," they said, "life has turned bitter. Nothing satisfies. I lost my job, argued with my brother, and now I spill more tears than tea. I see emptiness and loss everywhere."

Master Lin nodded and motioned for the traveler to sit. He prepared the tea slowly—washing the leaves, warming the cup. At last, he poured.

The traveler peered into the cup and frowned.

"It's only half full."

Master Lin smiled. "So it is."

The traveler sighed. "Why not fill it to the top?"

Without a word, Master Lin poured more until the cup brimmed. When the traveler lifted it, hot tea spilled over and burned their fingers.

"Ow!"

Master Lin placed a cool cloth on the table and spoke gently: "Some cups are best half full. Not because life withholds—but because space allows room for breath, for gratitude, for peace."

The traveler stared into the steam. "But what if I lose more? What if the cup empties completely?"

Master Lin refilled it halfway again. Then he asked, "If the cup is empty . . . is that truly the end?"

The traveler hesitated. "It feels like the end."

Master Lin nodded. "But it is also a beginning. Emptiness is not absence. It is invitation—to become curious, to look again, to see Spirit at work in the space itself. You are always at choice. Will you see what is missing—or what is waiting?"

The traveler breathed deeply. For the first time in weeks, they smiled.

"Then I will drink what is given . . . and trust that the cup won't stay empty for long."

Contemplation

1. When life feels empty, where does your attention go—toward loss or toward possibility?
2. What spaces in your life are inviting gratitude instead of fear?
3. Can you welcome the pause, the in-between, as sacred?

Affirmation

I welcome the space between what was and what will be.

I trust that emptiness is not lack, but preparation.

I see what is present, not what is missing.

I drink what is given and make room for what flows next.

Spirit fills my life—even in quiet, unseen ways.

When We Rise

There once lived a wayfinder named Agiren who studied sacred texts and often spoke of Spirit's wisdom. He sat each day beneath a great banyan tree on the tallest hill above the village, whispering mantras from dawn until dusk.

He was known for his stillness, his certainty, and his eloquent prayers. "Trust the Divine," he would say. "All is unfolding in perfect order."

One year, the rains did not come.

The river shrank. The trees grew brittle. The ground cracked open beneath the village. And while the villagers grew anxious, Agiren prayed harder.

He quoted scriptures. He invoked healing. He chanted the many names of God.

As the drought deepened, some villagers left in search of water. Others stayed, trusting the mendicant's devotion would bring relief. Then one afternoon, a fire sparked in the dry brush. Within minutes, the flames leapt toward the homes on the edge of the village.

A young water girl ran breathless to the hill. "Please," she cried, "we need help! Buckets! Anything! If the fire spreads, we will lose everything!"

But the wayfinder only raised his voice, lifting his arms to the sky. "The Divine will provide. I am in communion," he said.

The fire raged through the night. The village was reduced to ash.

The next morning, the wayfinder descended from the hill. Among the scorched ruins, he found the girl sitting where her tent once stood. She turned to him, smoke in her hair, soot on her face.

"Master," she said quietly, "I believe in prayer. I believe in Spirit. But are we not also asked to rise? To carry the water? To be the hands of the Divine?"

Agiren looked back toward the banyan tree on the hill, high above and separated from the charred lands below. And something shifted within him.

Perhaps intention without action is . . . not faith, but avoidance.

He turned to the girl, eyes softening. "I was wrong," he said. "I left you to carry the burden while I stayed in silence. Please forgive me. If you'll allow it, I would like to help rebuild what was lost."

Agiren dropped to his knees beside her, lifted the first stone, and began rebuilding the village—this time, with open hands and an open heart.

Contemplation

1. Do I sometimes confuse spiritual practice with spiritual passivity?
2. Is there an area of my life where Spirit is asking me to rise, move, or take compassionate action?
3. Is there someone I've wronged—intentionally or not—who deserves my apology and amends?

Affirmation

I honor Spirit not only through prayer, but through action.
Each day, I rise to be the hands and heart of the Divine.
I have the courage to admit when I've caused harm.
Making amends is a sacred part of my healing.
I walk with humility, and I rebuild in love.

The Weary Man and the Awkward Dog

There once was a weary man who lived on the outskirts of a village in a small bungalow. He had lived a full life—married, raised a family, and run a small business that had employed many villagers.

But time had slowed him down. His partner had passed, his children had moved away, and he had closed his business. His once-thriving garden now grew wild, for he no longer had the energy to tend it.

Beyond the village, the country was in turmoil. People wanted more and more but spent less and less time with one another. Neighbor against neighbor.

Family against family. Greed seemed to flood the land like a rising tide.

One afternoon, as the man sat on his front porch, a traveler passed by carrying a peculiar little dog. The dog had mismatched eyes—one blue, one brown—and an awkward stance. Strange markings and old scars covered his body.

The traveler, weary from the road, offered the dog in exchange for a bit of bread. The man, not knowing what else to do, accepted.

From that day on, the dog never left his side. They moved through the quiet rhythms of the man's days together.

Each morning, the dog would dance a silly jig for his breakfast, then sit by his new companion as he sipped his morning coffee.

The man chuckled to himself. How can one rather funny-looking dog bring me such joy? The dog, as if understanding, tilted his head and barked in reply.

One day, feeling lighter than he had in years, the man pulled out his old harmonica. As he played, the dog pranced around, spinning and jumping—a mismatched, joyful blur. The man laughed—a deep, belly laugh he hadn't heard from himself in a long time.

Then, one morning, as he sipped his coffee, an idea came to him. Perhaps music, like joy, is best shared.

With the dog trotting beside him, he wandered down into the village and stood at the street corner. He lifted his harmonica and played, while the awkward dog twirled and hopped beside him.

At first, the villagers hurried past, lost in their own concerns. But the man didn't mind.

He played because it felt good to play, and the dog danced because it felt good to dance. There was no need for anything more.

For several weeks, a bread maker on her way to work took notice. One morning, she entertained a curious thought:

How can one man and his awkward little dog bring me such joy?

As she continued on her way, she pondered that thought and smiled. Suddenly, an inspired idea came to her—perhaps joy, like bread, was meant to be shared.

Contemplation

1. What simple joys in your life are you overlooking or underestimating?
2. How might one small act of lightness or presence ripple outward from you?
3. In what way can you pass joy forward today?

Affirmation

I notice the beauty already within my life.
I choose to share the good I have been given.
Joy multiplies through simple, generous acts.
My presence can uplift even a stranger's day.
The smallest light can brighten the world.

The Ferryman and the River of Time

A traveler arrived at the banks of a wide and winding river, eager to reach the great city beyond. There, waiting at the dock, was an old ferryman, his wooden boat gently rocking with the current.

"Take me across," the traveler said, climbing aboard. "But please, let's go quickly. I don't have time to waste."

The ferryman smiled, pushed off from shore, and let the current take them. The boat glided smoothly, the oars barely needed.

The traveler, impatient, watched the winding river with frustration. "Why aren't you rowing harder? The city is miles away. If we don't move faster, it will take all day!"

The ferryman dipped an oar into the water and steered effortlessly around a bend. "Tell me," he said, "how long does it take this river to reach the sea?"

The traveler frowned. "I suppose . . . it depends. Some parts move swiftly, others get caught in bends and rocks. It may take days, weeks, maybe even months."

The ferryman nodded. "And yet, the river does not concern itself with time. It simply flows. Whether fast or slow, it always reaches the sea."

The traveler crossed his arms. "That may be fine for a river, but I don't have the luxury of waiting. The city is ahead, and I need to be there soon."

The ferryman knelt by the water, trailing his hand in the current. "You think time is fixed, but it is not. It stretches and bends, just like the river. When you struggle against it, it slows. When you fight for control, you only exhaust yourself. But when you trust the flow, you move as quickly as you are meant to."

He picked up an oar and lightly dipped it in the water, shifting the boat just enough to ride the natural currents. The river carried them forward with ease. The traveler, now watching the water instead of fighting it, realized the truth:

What seems slow when you resist . . . becomes effortless when you align.

And long before nightfall, the great city appeared on the horizon.

Contemplation

1. Where in your life are you struggling against time instead of trusting its flow?
2. How do you experience time differently when you're present versus when you're anxious?
3. How might your day feel different if you trusted that you're exactly where you need to be?

Affirmation

I release the need to rush.
I align with the natural flow of life.
Time expands when I trust.
Every moment carries me forward.
I arrive exactly when I am meant to.

The Bridge Over the Ocean

Three pilgrims, each wise in his own way, set out on a sacred journey to a distant land, carrying satchels filled with the sacred books of their most treasured traditions. One day, they arrived at the edge of a vast, seemingly impassable ocean. Staring into the endless horizon, their hearts grew heavy with uncertainty. They knew their destiny awaited on the far shore, but no clear path lay before them.

At that moment, each pilgrim called out in the language of his faith.

The first cried out, "Jesus, be my guide."
The second bowed, "Brahman, light my path."
The third lifted his hands, "Allah, grant me strength."

To their wonder, a bridge began to appear—a luminous, shifting pathway stretching gracefully across the waters. As they stood at its entrance, the travelers exchanged puzzled looks and soon began to argue.

"It is my God who provides," each insisted.

Their voices grew louder, discord and anger filling the air. Then, from the shadows, a figure emerged—an old sage dressed in tattered robes. He raised his hand, and a quiet authority silenced their debate.

"Tell me," the sage asked, "have you ever tried to capture the ocean in a jar?"

The pilgrims shook their heads, for they knew that such a thing was impossible.

The sage continued, "You are guided by a power far greater than even this ocean—limitless, ever-changing, and beyond capture. To truly know it, you must release your attachment to a name and surrender to its mystery."

The three travelers fell silent. Then, as one, they turned toward the bridge and took their first step—together.

Contemplation

1. What jar are you using to contain the vastness of Spirit?
2. Have you ever felt divided from others by beliefs, even when the destination was the same?
3. What might shift if you focused on the spiritual essence rather than names or labels?

Affirmation

I walk with others toward the same horizon.
I release the need to name the mystery.
Spirit flows beyond any limitations.
The mystery is wider than any path.
I trust the bridge beneath my feet.

THE JOYFUL HEART AND THE HUMMINGBIRD

There once was a seeker named Ahyoka, born with a deep knowing in her chest. Her guide was not a map or a compass, but her heart—a quiet, steady rhythm pulsing with the voice of Spirit.

Whenever the world became noisy or unclear, Ahyoka would place her hand over her heart. She'd breathe. She'd listen. In stillness, she'd find her way again. She had learned to calm her thoughts, reexamine her beliefs, and realign with love.

But one day, Ahyoka stood at a crossroads. She was faced with a decision about which path to take over the mountains.

Her people each offered their voice—opinions, doubts, expectations.

"Stay on this path."
"Be more patient."
"You just need to see it differently."

Ahyoka quickly became overwhelmed with their voices. She closed her eyes and touched her heart.

It spoke clearly: follow your joy.

The message was not one of urgency or fear, but quietly centered—like a steady knowing she recognized deep within.

Yet still, she doubted. "Maybe I need to reflect more. Maybe I should just shift my mindset and tell a new story."

She began questioning what, in stillness, she already knew to be true. And yet her heart pulsed with clarity—not in desperation, but in a pull toward excitement.

A red hummingbird swooped from the sky and hovered before her. "Why do you hesitate?" it asked. "Fear contracts, but love expands. Follow your heart."

Ahyoka listened. The decision no longer felt threatening. It felt true. She turned toward the path on her right and smiled—not because she was sure of every step, but because she was certain of herself.

She took the path of her heart—not to escape, but to expand.

Not from fear, but from love.

Not for others, but for her own truth.

And with each step, the wind quieted behind her.

Contemplation

1. When faced with a decision, do you pause to listen to your heart before absorbing others' opinions?
2. When have you dismissed a quiet inner knowing and followed someone else's story instead?
3. What would it feel like to trust your heart completely—even if the path feels uncertain or misunderstood?

Affirmation

My heart is wise, quiet, and clear.
I listen lightly to the opinions of others
I choose love over fear.
Joy is not indulgence—it is guidance.
I walk the path of my own truth.

The Fisher Boy's Story

In a quiet fishing village, a boy named Renyu had heard of a master fisherman who lived at the tip of the island—a man whose nets were never empty, whose lines always carried a fine catch.

Determined to learn his secret, Renyu sought out the old man and pleaded, "Teach me to be a master fisherman."

The fisherman smiled and handed him a fishing line. Without a word, he chose a shimmering lure, cast it into the sea, and waited. Soon, the line tugged. With a gentle pull, the master reeled in a gleaming fish, its silver scales flashing in the sunlight.

Renyu's eyes widened. "How did you know that would work?"

The fisherman unhooked the fish and said, "Fish glitter and attract the light. Each seeks the same."

Renyu reached into his tackle box. His fingers brushed against a small, timeworn lure—the finest he owned. It had been passed down through generations, a treasure once held by his father, and his father before him. Though its edges were worn and its colors had faded, it carried the weight of tradition and respect. Surely, this would bring in the best catch.

With quiet reverence, he fastened it to his hook, cast his line into the water, and waited.

The boy sat for hours, watching as the master fisherman pulled in fish after fish. His own line remained still, untouched. As the sun dipped low, he only caught a feisty crab—but not a single fish.

Frustrated, he turned to the fisherman. "Master, how is it that we are fishing in the same ocean and having two very different experiences?"

The fisherman nodded. "The sea is vast, but only what we cast is drawn back to us."

Contemplation

1. What lures are you casting into life—through your thoughts, beliefs, or actions—and what do they attract?
2. Are you holding onto traditions or ideas that no longer serve you, simply because they were passed down?
3. How can you become more aware of the unseen currents shaping your experiences?

Affirmation

I cast into life with intention and clarity.
My thoughts and words shape what returns to me.
I no longer send out what no longer serves.
I release the weight of old patterns.
What I attract reflects what I believe I'm worthy to receive.

A Tale of Two Gardens

There was once a wise farmer who had two sons. When they came of age, he gave each a plot of land and a sack of seeds.

"Tend your land well," he told them. "Learn from it, and it will teach you."

The older son, confident in his beliefs, planted his seeds in neat, straight rows. He cleared the soil of rocks, weeds, and insects. "Nothing will harm my seeds; they will grow proud and strong," he said. He spent his days pulling dandelions, thistles, and clover, keeping his field in perfect order.

The younger son, watching his brother, tried to imitate his process. But while clearing rocks, he noticed dandelions blooming nearby. Their golden heads sparkled in the sun. He paused as butterflies and bees gathered around the flowers, and ladybugs nestled among the leaves. He plucked a leaf and tasted it.

Many call these weeds, he thought, but maybe they have a purpose. He decided to let them stay where nature had placed them.

As summer passed, the elder son's garden grew tall and rigid. The large plants drank deeply from the soil, but their uniformity attracted imbalance. Grasshoppers arrived in droves, devouring the crops.

Panicked, the older son sprayed heavy poisons. The grasshoppers scattered, but without predators, aphids came—clinging to the leaves, draining them of life.

Meanwhile, the younger son's garden thrived in quiet harmony. Tall corn shaded the beans. Dandelions attracted ladybugs, who fed on aphids. Clover enriched the soil. The garden worked together—each plant, insect, and odd plant playing a role.

When autumn came, the father returned. Seeing the two fields, the older son cried out: "Why has my brother's garden flourished while mine has failed? I planted the best seeds. I removed every weed. I struck down every insect."

The farmer smiled. "My son, you saw only what you believed necessary and rejected what you did not understand. But the land does not work alone."

The older son looked again—really looked. He saw the balance. The beauty. The wild, living network his brother had embraced.

The father rested a hand on his shoulder. "What if your certainty has caused you to no longer see?"

Contemplation

1. Where in your life are you removing what you don't understand instead of exploring its purpose?
2. What beauty or wisdom might you be rejecting because it doesn't look the way you expected?
3. What would it feel like to loosen your grip on control and allow Spirit to show you the deeper order beneath the chaos?

Affirmation

I release the need to control the process.
I trust that Spirit works in both order and wildness.
What I once rejected may hold unseen wisdom.
I soften my lead and let wisdom reveal itself.
Abundance grows when I allow all things their place.

The Weaver and the Light

In a quiet village by the sea, there lived a woman named Thea. She was known for weaving the most intricate and beautiful tapestries, her hands moving effortlessly across the loom. People traveled from far and wide to see her work, believing she possessed a rare gift.

One day, a young girl named Lucia came to visit. She had long admired Thea and wished to learn the secret of her craft.

"How do you weave with such grace?" she asked. "Your hands never hesitate, and your patterns seem to emerge as if from the air itself."

Thea smiled and invited Lucia to sit beside her. "Come, place your hands on the loom," she said.

Lucia obeyed, but as she worked, she found herself hesitating. She overthought each movement, second-guessed her choices, and worried about making a mistake. The threads tangled, and her frustration grew.

Thea gently placed her hand over Lucia's. "Do you see the light?" she asked.

Lucia looked around. Sunlight filtered through the leaves of an old olive tree outside the window, shifting as the breeze moved its branches. The golden beams danced along the wooden floor, illuminating parts of the loom while others remained in shadow.

"The light does not ask where to go," Thea continued. "It moves freely, knowing it is always guided. My weaving is no different. I do not force the pattern—I align with the movement of Spirit, and it flows through me."

Lucia looked down at the tangled threads and sighed. "But how do I trust like that? My mind keeps interfering."

Thea smiled. "You must let go of trying to control the tapestry and instead focus on your connection to the light."

Lucia closed her eyes and took a deep breath, allowing herself to feel the warmth of the sun on her skin, to notice the way the light moved without effort—always present, always illuminating. She opened her eyes and touched the threads again—this time, moving in that middle place, without fear or hesitation.

Over time, her weaving became effortless, a dance of presence rather than effort. She no longer sought perfection but trusted that each thread was placed in perfection.

Years later, when people admired her work, she would only smile and say, "It is not I who weaves—it is the light through my hands."

Contemplation

1. Where in your life are you trying too hard to control the outcome?
2. What is your personal 'tangled thread'—the doubt or fear that disrupts your flow?
3. How can you practice aligning with the light instead of forcing the pattern?

Affirmation

I release the need to control the pattern.
I align with the light that moves through all things.
Spirit flows when I quiet the mind and open the heart.
My hands remember what my soul already knows.
The pattern unfolds through presence, not force.

The Traveler and the Compass

A weary traveler trudged through a dense forest, burdened by the weight of his journey. In one hand, he clutched a long rope, sturdy and well-worn, a tool of security and preparedness. In the other, he gripped a collection of tools—each useful in its own way, though growing heavier with every step. Every item felt essential, each chosen to protect him from the unknown.

As he pressed deep into the wilderness, the trees thickened, the path winding and uncertain. Then, just ahead on the ground, he spotted something gleaming in the dim light—a golden compass. He knelt, eyes widening as the needle pointed unwaveringly toward his destination. Relief flooded his chest. This was exactly what he had needed all along.

But as he reached down to pick it up, he hesitated. Both hands were full.

His fingers tightened around the rope and the tools he had carried for so long. He considered letting go of the tools—but what if he needed them? What if a challenge arose that only they could solve?

He glanced at the rope—its fibers frayed in places yet still strong, a symbol of safety when climbing to great heights. Letting it go felt unthinkable.

He stood frozen, heart pounding. To take the compass, he had to let go of something.

Minutes passed. The wind whispered through the trees, rustling the leaves like hushed voices urging him forward. But he remained still, unwilling to release what had once seemed indispensable.

In the end, he turned away, stepping back into the forest—his hands full, his path unclear.

Contemplation

1. What in your life feels essential but may be weighing you down?
2. Where have you hesitated to embrace something new because of what you're unwilling to release?
3. What might the "compass" in your life be right now—and what must you let go of to grasp it?

Affirmation

I trust that what I need will show up when I'm ready.
I let go of what's no longer helpful, even if it once was.
My hands are open. I make space for what's next.
I take one clear step at a time.
The path may twist, but I walk it with trust.

THE KING AND HIS THREE SONS

There once was a wise king who ruled over a prosperous land. As he grew older, he worried about which of his three sons would inherit the throne.

The eldest, Dorin, saw only lack and danger. He believed the kingdom was fragile, that enemies lurked in every shadow, and that ruin was inevitable. Fear gripped his heart, and it tightened his vision. "Prepare for the worst," he would warn, "or we shall all suffer." The king noted that he was quick to judge and act.

The second son, Lucian, was an eternal optimist. He believed all things worked out for the best, no matter what. He lived with his eyes only on the sun, refusing to see the storms forming behind him. "There is nothing to fear," he would say. "Life will always be kind to us." He saw only the best in every situation.

But the youngest, Sorin, was odd indeed. The king often wondered if he had the strength to deal with the challenges of life. Sorin neither expected misfortune nor assumed the best—and often seemed quiet. He neither shrank in fear nor leaped in judgment. He observed and withheld most of his opinions. At times, Sorin seemed to step back and watch even himself from a distance.

One day, word spread that a great storm was coming—one unlike any the kingdom had ever seen. The king summoned his sons and asked what should be done.

Dorin, consumed by fear, ordered the castle to be barricaded. "This is the end," he declared. "Stockpile the grain, shut the gates, and prepare for famine. We may never recover."

Lucian, lost in blind optimism, laughed. "Why worry? The storm will pass, the sun will shine again, and no harm will come to us." He called for a festival that very night so that they could dance in the rain!

But Sorin stepped outside. He studied the sky, felt the shifting winds, and listened to the whispers of the land. He saw the river rising, the soil softening, and birds fleeing inland. He noticed a flicker of fear—and even excitement—within himself.

He returned and said, "The storm is real, but fear will not save us, nor will ignoring it. Right action comes not from contraction or denial, but from love—love for our people, our land, and our future. We must prepare, but wisely."

The king, impressed, asked what should be done.

Sorin advised moving livestock to higher ground, reinforcing bridges, and storing food safely—not in panic, but with thoughtful care. He assured the people that all would end well and encouraged them to sing while they prepared.

When the storm arrived, it was indeed powerful. Winds howled, rains flooded the fields, and the rivers swelled—but the kingdom endured.

Dorin, locked in his barricaded tower, suffocated in his own fear, unable to see that the storm had passed. Lucian, caught mid-celebration, was unprepared and swept away. But those who followed Sorin's guidance—who neither shrank in fear nor abandoned wisdom for blind faith—weathered the storm.

When the sun rose again, the king turned to his people and declared, "The throne does not belong to those who fear, nor to those who ignore—but to those who are willing to see."

Contemplation

1. How do you typically respond to life's storms—with fear, blind optimism, or quiet observation?
2. Where are you over-preparing in fear or ignoring potential challenges?
3. How can you cultivate the ability to 'see' rather than react?

Affirmation

I face challenges with calm awareness.
I release fear and resist false certainty.
I watch with open eyes and a quiet mind.
I observe myself with compassion and honesty.
From this still place, wise action arises.

The Still Water and the Ripple

In a quiet mountain village, a wise woman named Amara lived by the edge of a still lake. Villagers often sought her counsel, and one day, a young man named Lior arrived, his brow furrowed with worry.

"The village is unraveling," he said. "Fear is spreading like wildfire. People fight over what they once shared freely. I try to speak reason, but no one listens."

Amara nodded gently and motioned toward the lake. "Come. Let me show you something."

At the water's edge, she handed him a small stone. "Throw this into the lake," she said.

Lior tossed it in. They both watched as a single ripple widened in perfect circles, calm and steady, until it touched the farthest shores.

"One quiet motion," she said, "and the whole lake feels it."

Then, Amara picked up a stick and stirred the water forcefully. Waves broke the surface, swirling in confusion.

"Now, throw another stone."

Lior obeyed, but this time, the stone's ripple was lost—swallowed in the turmoil.

"The lake is like the world in chaos," Amara said softly. "When your heart is stirred by fear, even your clearest words are drowned. But when you are still—when you embody love—your presence carries farther than you realize."

Lior gazed at the water, the truth settling within him. He had tried to change others by force—by stirring the surface—when he was called to become the stillness instead.

From that day forward, Lior stopped trying to be heard. He became still, listened and deeply present.

And over time, the village changed—not because he shouted over the fear, but because his quiet presence was felt.

Contemplation

1. When have you tried to force change, only to feel unheard or ignored?
2. What emotions or beliefs ripple outward from you into the world—are they rooted in fear, urgency, or peace?
3. How can you cultivate stillness and clarity within yourself, even when surrounded by chaos?

Refined Affirmation

I choose stillness over force.

I trust that change begins within me.

My clarity and peace ripple outward, even in chaos.

I release control and step into loving presence.

Rooted in stillness, I become a presence for good.

Voyage of Grateful Words

Two women, Delia and Lia, boarded a great passenger ship bound for another land. Both had left behind all they knew, carrying only their hopes and uncertainties across the vast ocean.

One night, as a violent storm raged, the sea swallowed the ship whole, leaving them adrift on a broken raft amid endless waves.

Delia sat hunched, her arms wrapped tightly around herself. "This is the end," she whispered. "We are lost, and no one will find us."

Lia, though weary, lifted her face toward the sky. "Do not fear," she said aloud, her voice steady against the wind. "Though this night is dark, the sun will rise again. I see a great ship coming for us, and I know we will be saved."

Delia shook her head. "Foolish hope and strong words will not keep us alive. We have lost everything—our families, our homes, our future."

But Lia did not waver. She spoke into the night, her words deliberate and unwavering. "I give thanks for this journey. I give thanks for the life I have lived. I had a loving husband, a home filled with laughter, and children who brought me joy. And even now, I am grateful—for the breath in my lungs, for this raft beneath me, for the stars that shine above us."

The storm grew fiercer, tossing them like leaves upon the sea. A monstrous wave crashed down, splintering their raft and pulling them apart. When the waters settled, Delia was gone, lost beneath the waves.

Lia clung to a single wooden plank, her body shivering from cold, yet her heart remained steady. Perhaps I will not survive, she murmured, but for this one thing, I am grateful—I am here, and the moon keeps me company.

As dawn broke, golden light stretched across the waves, and in the distance, a ship appeared. Lia barely had the strength to lift her head, but soon she felt strong hands pulling her aboard.

Gasping, she turned to the captain. "How did you ever find me?"

The captain smiled. "The sun caught something glimmering in the water. We almost passed you by, but the light guided us."

Lia looked down at her torn clothes, her bare hands.

"But I have nothing—no luggage, no jewelry. I let it all sink."

The captain smiled. "You kept the one thing that matters—your words of gratitude."

Contemplation

1. What words are you speaking into your life—are they rooted in faith or in fear?
2. When faced with uncertainty, do you cling to doubt like Delia, or surrender with trust like Lia?
3. What language are you holding onto that may need to be released to guide you toward your highest good?

Affirmation

My words are stars guiding my ship through the dark.
They lead me across unknown waters with trust and grace.
I speak into the waves with clarity and faith.
What I release flows back to me in divine timing.
I let love be the current that carries me toward all that is good.

The Hunter's Strength

Once, there was a great Hunter known throughout the land for his unmatched skill and bravery. He had faced mountain lions, wolves, and fierce beasts, always emerging victorious. His reputation stretched far and wide. He walked with pride, certain that his power and determination made him invincible.

One season, word spread through the village of a mighty grizzly bear roaming the mountains. The villagers spoke in hushed voices of its unmatched size and ferocity, warning all who dared venture into its domain. The Hunter, thrilled by the challenge, set out on a relentless pursuit, determined to claim his greatest trophy.

For weeks, he tracked the beast—finding its massive claw marks on trees, seeing the wreckage left at nearby farms—but never glimpsing it. Frustrated, he began to pray for a chance to face the bear, to prove himself once again.

Then, one day, he met a villager running in terror down the mountain path.

"The bear! The grizzly is near the summit! It nearly took my life!" the man gasped before fleeing in the opposite direction.

The Hunter's heart pounded with excitement. At last, the moment had come. He gripped his weapon, steadied himself, and marched forward, his confidence unwavering.

At the mountain's peak, he rounded a bend—and there it was.

The bear stood before him, far larger and more powerful than he had ever imagined. Its fur was thick, its muscles rippled with strength, and its eyes burned with anger.

Without hesitation, the Hunter drew his bow and released an arrow. The shot struck the bear's hind leg, and it let out a deafening roar, shaking the very ground. The beast turned toward him—not weakened, but enraged.

The Hunter fired again, piercing its shoulder. Still, the beast did not falter. Instead, it charged, faster than anything he had ever seen.

Panic flickered. He had never faced a force like this. He reached for another arrow, but before he could nock it, the bear was upon him.

The two clashed in a violent struggle. Though strong, the Hunter was outmatched. Every time he pushed, the bear pushed harder. Its claws tore through his skin. Its teeth sank into his flesh. Blood stained the ground.

Exhaustion overtook him, and a realization surfaced: he had met a power that could not be overpowered.

And in that moment, he yielded.

He stopped resisting. His body went limp. He dropped his weapon and let his breath slow.

Lying beneath the beast, he turned his gaze upward and accepted what was. He noticed the pine trees swaying gently above him, the sunlight breaking through the clouds, the distant call of a bird in the valley below. A deep peace settled over him as he thought of his village, his wife, his child, and the wonder of his life.

Indeed, he had lived a well-lived life.

As if sensing the shift, the great beast lost interest. It let out a final huff and sauntered away, disappearing into the trees.

The Hunter, weak and bloodied, lay motionless—not in defeat, but in understanding. He had believed that power came from force, that victory required domination. But now, as he watched the bear vanish into the forest, he knew the truth:

It was in yielding that he endured.

Days later, the villagers found him on the mountain, barely alive. They nursed his wounds, and as he healed, he shared his story—not of conquest, but of surrender.

For all his strength and skill, it was not his weapons, nor his will, that had saved him.

It was his willingness to let go.

Panic flickered. He had never faced a force like this. He reached for another arrow, but before he could nock it, the bear was upon him.

The two clashed in a violent struggle. Though strong, the Hunter was outmatched. Every time he pushed, the bear pushed harder. Its claws tore through his skin. Its teeth sank into his flesh. Blood stained the ground.

Exhaustion overtook him, and a realization surfaced: he had met a power that could not be overpowered.

And in that moment, he yielded.

He stopped resisting. His body went limp. He dropped his weapon and let his breath slow.

Lying beneath the beast, he turned his gaze upward and accepted what was. He noticed the pine trees swaying gently above him, the sunlight breaking through the clouds, the distant call of a bird in the valley below. A deep peace settled over him as he thought of his village, his wife, his child, and the wonder of his life.

Indeed, he had lived a well-lived life.

As if sensing the shift, the great beast lost interest. It let out a final huff and sauntered away, disappearing into the trees.

The Hunter, weak and bloodied, lay motionless—not in defeat, but in understanding. He had believed that power came from force, that victory required domination. But now, as he watched the bear vanish into the forest, he knew the truth:

It was in yielding that he endured.

Days later, the villagers found him on the mountain, barely alive. They nursed his wounds, and as he healed, he shared his story—not of conquest, but of surrender.

For all his strength and skill, it was not his weapons, nor his will, that had saved him.

It was his willingness to let go.

Contemplation

1. Where in your life are you resisting instead of allowing?
2. What are you afraid will happen if you let go?
3. Is your fear truly protecting you—or preventing growth and peace?

Affirmation

I recognize that some things cannot be controlled.
I release resistance and allow life to unfold.
I surrender to what is, and in yielding, I find strength.
I trust that letting go creates space for peace and growth.
I align with the deeper wisdom moving through my life.

For Every Seed, a Purpose

*O*nce, in a quiet patch of earth, a small seed lay buried beneath the soil. It did not know what kind of seed it was, but it was certain it had a spectacular purpose.

As the rains softened the ground, the seed sent out its first tender sprout. Looking around, it saw mighty trees towering above and thought, Perhaps I am meant to be like them—strong, tall, unshakable.

But just as it stretched upward, a passing traveler unknowingly stepped on it, bending its fragile stem. The seedling ached with disappointment. I will never be tall now. What good am I if I cannot be a tree?

Yet, even in its sorrow, the seedling found something unexpected—it was resilient. Though not strong like a tree, it continued to grow.

I may not be a stately tree, but surely there is some purpose for me.

The seedling continued to grow and developed broad leaves. It noticed a cluster of golden sunflowers stretching high into the sky. Perhaps I am meant to be like them—radiant, admired, reaching for the heavens. Surely, if I were as beautiful as a sunflower, everyone would honor me.

And when its own buds began to form, it felt certain it had found its purpose.

But when the first bud finally opened, it was nothing like the glorious sunflowers across the field. The bloom was simple, fleeting—nothing grand. I will never be so magnificent. What good am I if I cannot be a thing of beauty?

So, it let go of its longing. Instead of reaching for the sky, it stretched its vines along the earth, casting broad leaves and simple flowers. I must be content with what I am, it thought.

One by one, the blossoms opened—only to wither by nightfall. And then, even the dull petals fell to the ground, leaving behind small, lumpy bumps where they once bloomed.

At least I am not ugly, it reasoned. But as days passed, the small bumps swelled. More appeared where the fallen flowers had been. The bumps grew to an incredible size, and their weight forced them to the ground.

The plant sighed. Perhaps this is all I was meant to be.

One scorching afternoon, a group of weary travelers stumbled upon the plant and its strange, cylindrical pods. Parched, they plucked several of the melons and lifted them toward the sky. They gave thanks, then sliced them open to reveal a glowing center—rich golden-orange, like the heart of the sun. With the first bite, sweet juice ran down their chins, and something stirred within them. Warmth returned to their limbs. Color flushed back into their faces. They laughed. They wept. They were whole again.

At last, the plant understood.

I was never meant to stand tall. I was never meant to be a thing of beauty. But I was always meant to be of service.

Contemplation

1. What qualities have emerged in you through challenges you once saw as setbacks?
2. How do you respond when life doesn't unfold the way you expect?
3. In what quiet, unassuming ways might you already be of service to others?

Affirmation

I honor the path that shaped me.

I release the need to compare or prove.

What I offer is enough—more than enough.

I grow into service without striving.

I am already a gift to the world.

The Pilgrim's Journey

A devout pilgrim set out on a long journey to reach the Sacred Summit, believing that at its peak, he would find ultimate wisdom. He had studied the ancient texts, and they all spoke of the one great truth—that truth was kept in a great castle on the holiest of high holy mountains.

And so, with great faith, a journal in hand, he began his climb.

After many days, the pilgrim arrived at a great temple carved into the mountainside. Inside, scholars debated philosophy and recited sacred scriptures. Their words were vast, their knowledge deep, and he decided to stay.

For many years, the pilgrim sat among them, listening intently, taking notes, hoping to grasp the wisdom he sought.

But something troubled him.

Each speaker claimed to know the truth, yet they all spoke differently. They argued, revised, and contradicted one another. The more the pilgrim listened, the less certain he became.

Finally, he asked one of the elders, "Which is the truth?"

The elder smiled. "Words can describe the path, but they are not the journey."

Though the scholars spoke with certainty, the more he listened, the more the truth seemed to slip through his grasp. Seeking something beyond words, he set out climbing once more.

Higher up the mountain, the air grew thin, and the voices of the scholars faded. The pilgrim came upon a small cave, where an old hermit sat in stillness. Unlike the temple, there were no books, no teachings—only silence.

The pilgrim bowed and sat beside the hermit, waiting for instruction. But none came.

Hours passed. Then days. Then years. The hermit only smiled and remained silent.

At first, the pilgrim cherished the absence of conflicting voices, believing he had found something deeper.

But over time, a quiet question began to rise within him: was there more than silence?

One morning, as the light streamed through the cave entrance, he realized—he longed for something more. The light beckoned him to continue.

He stumbled to his feet and returned to his ascent. The terrain began to thin, the trees no longer obscured his view, and the sky stretched wide before him.

At last, the pilgrim reached the peak. He expected a temple, a wise master, a sacred inscription—something to mark his arrival.

But there was no one and no thing. Only a large boulder, a twisted cedar, and scattered grass.

He was alone.

Disheartened, the pilgrim whispered, "Is this it? Have I traveled all this way for nothing?"

He sighed and let go of the questions that had carried him here.

He smelled the scent of the scrub pine gathered a few feet away.

He tasted the sweetness of wildflower blossoms carried by the breeze.

He heard the wind circling the peak, whispering through the stones.

He saw the vast landscape, stretching beyond what words could hold.

He felt the warmth of the sun on his skin, alive and moving.

And in that moment, he sensed a oneness with all that surrounded him.

He smiled.

The answer was not a destination. He carried the answer with him all along.

Contemplation

1. Have you placed your faith in a specific teacher, tradition, or holy place, believing it holds the answer—rather than recognizing that wisdom is already within you?
2. Are you still searching for truth in words or silence, rather than engaging fully with presence?
3. How can you practice "listening" with all your senses—seeing, hearing, touching, smelling, and tasting—the way the pilgrim did at the summit?

Affirmation

I walk in search of truth, but I carry it within me.
Every step reveals what I already know.
I release the need for perfect words or perfect silence.
I open to the wisdom of this moment.
I listen with all that I am.

The Well Between Them

There was once a village where all drew water from a single, sacred well.

Each morning, two women walked the winding path that led to it:

Dilara, with a calm step and an open heart, and Anwar, with furrowed brow and quick feet.

They both carried urns—wide, hand-molded clay. They both reached the well just after sunrise. They both lowered their ropes and drew from the same depth.

But what they brought home was never the same.

Dilara approached the well with quiet reverence. She gave thanks before drawing. Sometimes she sang:

"Thank you, Spirit, for the life you offer."

She let the rope down slowly, listening for the sound of water. She lifted it up with ease, never rushing, never doubting. Her urn always returned full—and light in her hands. The water sparkled. It stayed cool all day. She shared it freely. Her house was filled with laughter, plants, and peace.

Anwar, on the other hand, arrived each day with suspicion. She muttered about how others took too much. She worried the well would run dry.

"I'd better take extra—just in case."

She yanked the rope down, splashing, scraping. She hauled it back hard, bracing her feet. Her urn often returned half-filled or spilled on the path. The water warmed quickly. Sometimes it tasted like stone. She drank it alone, behind closed doors, and wondered why she was always thirsty.

One morning, Dilara arrived early and found Anwar already there, staring into the well.

Anwar turned to her and said,

"How is it you always leave smiling, while I carry the same water and never feel satisfied?"

Dilara set her urn down and said gently:

"We come to the same well, but we do not carry the same heart. The well gives what we bring to it."

Anwar looked away, ashamed.

But Dilara smiled and stepped closer.

"You are strong," she said. "Even when your heart is heavy, you return each day. That alone is worthy of blessing."

Anwar blinked. Something softened in her chest.

She lowered her rope again—this time slowly, gently. And when she drew it up, her urn was full. The water shimmered in the light.

Anwar looked at Dilara, startled.

"How did you—?"

Dilara only nodded.

"What we give, returns. Even kindness."

And from that day on, the well between them offered more than water.

Contemplation

1. In your life, how are you receiving what you give to it?
2. How might a small act of appreciation or kindness shift the way you receive from the world?
3. What are you willing to give today—not to earn something back, but to open the flow?

Affirmation

I approach life with gratitude and open hands.
What I bring is returned in unexpected grace.
I release fear and make space for flow.
Each act of kindness draws the deeper waters.
The well is never empty when my heart is full.

The Thing Itself

Long ago, all the people of the world lived in the same village. They worked together in harmony, each offering their gifts to the community. Over time, as each group tended to its own craft, they naturally developed different ways of seeing. Still, they lived in peace, bound together by a shared purpose.

One day, a young boy ran excitedly through the village, his voice full of wonder. "Come, come quickly! I have discovered something marvelous!"

Curious, the people followed him to the center of the village. There, standing tall and strong, was a great and glorious thing—its deep roots stretched into the earth, its thick trunk rose firm and unshaken, its broad canopy reached toward the sky, shimmering as the wind whispered through its small, tender leaves.

The villagers gasped. How had they not noticed its beauty before?

The boy turned to the nearest elder. "Tell me, what is this thing called?"

The elder smiled and placed a hand over his heart. "It is an *árbol*."

Before the boy could respond, another elder shook his head. "No, no. It is an *arbre!*"

A third scoffed. "You are both mistaken—it is called *Baum!*"

A fourth elder stepped in. "You are all wrong. We call it *mti*."

Then another: "*Shù*."

And another: "*Ki*."

One by one, each elder proclaimed the name in their own tongue: *derevo, shajara, pēṛ, árvore*.

The boy's excitement turned to confusion. His small hands clenched into fists. His eyes darted from one elder to the next as their voices grew louder, each insisting on their name.

At last, the boy threw his arms into the air. "But I don't understand!" he cried. "Does it not contain the same elements for each of you? The deep, rich roots that anchor it to the earth? The thick, wide trunk that stands strong? The broad, sweeping canopy that gives shade? The small, tender leaves that dance in the wind? Can we agree on it's essence?"

The elders fell silent. Some lowered their heads, others stroked their chins in thought.

Slowly, the boy stepped forward. He placed his small hand against the rough bark and whispered, "This thing does not care what we call it . . ."

And in that moment, they understood.

Contemplation

1. In what ways do you hold onto names, labels, or beliefs so tightly that you miss the essence of what truly is?
2. How can you practice seeing beyond words and differences to recognize the shared roots that connect us all?
3. If a name does not change the nature of something, where else in your life might you be mistaking identification for truth?

Affirmation

I look beyond names and labels to see what is real.
Essence speaks in silence, not in argument.
I trust what my heart knows before my mind defines.
What connects us is deeper than what divides us.
I stand in the presence of the Thing Itself.

The Mind and the Body

Once upon a time, there were two inseparable travelers—Mind and Body. They journeyed together through life, each playing its role.

Mind was brilliant. It could solve complex problems, craft eloquent sentences, and think its way through any challenge. It took pride in its ability to reason, strategize, and create solutions for anything that stood in its way. Mind believed that with enough effort and intelligence, no obstacle was too great.

Body, on the other hand, was strong and reliable. It could run great distances, lift heavy burdens, and endure the demands that Mind placed upon it. Body was a faithful companion, always carrying out Mind's wishes without question. But unlike Mind, Body had needs—hunger, rest, warmth, stillness. It would whisper these needs softly, yet Mind often ignored them, convinced that it knew better.

One day, as they traveled along a dusty road, they encountered a charming stranger. He was well-dressed, well-spoken, and his voice carried the weight of knowledge. He greeted them warmly and spoke in many tongues, weaving grand stories of kingdoms and power.

"I seek companions to help me build a magnificent city," the stranger said. "It will be a marvel of design, intellect, and ambition. It will be the greatest creation of our time. Join me, and together we shall build something eternal."

Mind was captivated. Here was someone who matched its intelligence—someone who spoke with elegance, reason, and vision. This was an opportunity to prove its worth, to build something truly grand.

Just as Mind was about to accept the stranger's offer, Body tightened. A deep, twisting knot formed in its center. Mind opened Body's mouth to respond, but no words came.

"What is this?" Mind demanded. "Why can I not speak? Why are you failing me now?"

But Body did not respond. It only stood firm—silent, unmoving. The knot deepened, the air around them grew thick, and an unshakable unease settled in.

"Oh, Body," Mind scolded. "You are always so sensitive, so demanding. Why can't you just let go and allow me to do this one great thing?"

But Body would not yield. Instead, it began to shake. The trembling spread through its limbs, its core, its very being.

Mind, overwhelmed by the unfamiliar sensation of silence and tension, hesitated. And in that hesitation, it chose—just this once—to listen.

Together, they turned and walked past the stranger.

As they walked away, the tingling sensation did not fade. It pulsed through them—waves of energy, goosebumps rippling across their skin. Mind, so used to understanding everything, found itself humbled by something it could not explain.

Days later, Body and Mind heard talk about a dangerous stranger in town who had caused much harm. Many of the villagers followed his lead blindly.

"I never saw the danger," Mind murmured. "But you did."

Body remained silent, its breath steady and sure.

And then, a quiet thought surfaced—not crafted, not reasoned, but felt.

"Perhaps there is an intelligence older than words. A knowing that does not come from thinking, but from something deeper—something woven into the fabric of being."

Mind let the thought settle. It did not try to wrestle with it, or reshape it into logic.

For the first time, it simply felt it.

Contemplation

1. Have you ever felt an unexplainable sensation in your body warning you about a situation before your mind understood why?
2. Do you trust your body's signals, or do you tend to override them with logic and reasoning?
3. How can you practice balancing your mind's intelligence with your body's wisdom in daily life?

Affirmation

I listen to the wisdom beneath thought.
My body speaks with ancient knowing.
I trust what I feel, even when I cannot explain it.
Balance is found in deep listening.
Mind and Body walk together as one.

The Drop and the Ocean

There once was a single drop of water resting peacefully in the vast embrace of the ocean. For ages, it felt the rhythmic rise and fall of the waves, knowing itself as part of something greater—never separate, never alone. It felt its reach far and wide.

One day, the warmth of the sun called to the drop, lifting it into the sky as mist. At first, the drop marveled at its newfound freedom, floating high above the cool, blue water. But as the winds carried it farther from the sea, a sense of insecurity crept in.

"Who am I? Do I really matter? What is my meaning?"

The drop drifted aimlessly, wrapped in uncertainty.

Soon it encountered another drop, arrogant and self-assured. "Look how I rise higher than you. I am grand, and you are nothing," it said. "I am certainly more powerful than you." The drop hesitated and began to question its own worth. It drifted in heavy clouds, jumping from one to the other, believing itself to be alone.

Then, in the stillness of a cool evening, a gentle breeze whispered:

"Remember who you are."

The drop began to see itself in all things. It recognized the other drops swirling in the mist, each carrying the same doubt, the same longing for home, the same essence as itself. It saw rivers below, winding their way back to the sea. It noticed the grand horizon and the radiance of the rising sun. Letting go of fear, it expanded into itself.

And finally, let go.

The drop fell as rain—not in loss, but in acceptance. It plopped down upon leaves, soaked into the earth, and traveled through roots, rich soil, and rivers until, at last, it rejoined the vastness of the ocean.

"I was never lost," the drop realized. "I only forgot where I belonged."

And from then on, whenever the sun lifted it skyward, the drop trusted the expanse of the sky. It did not resist. It did not doubt. It rested in the moment, knowing that no matter how far it traveled, it was always home.

Contemplation

1. Where in your life do you feel a sense of separation from others?
2. What happens when you stop resisting and allow yourself to trust the natural flow of life?
3. How does your perception shift when you remember your connection to something greater?

Affirmation

I remember who I am.
I am not alone—I am one with all that is.
Each soul I meet is another drop of the same sea.
Even in moments of doubt, I am part of the whole.
Wherever I go, I carry connection within me.

The Stranger at the Door

There was a man named Thomás who lived in a house at the edge of a dense forest. His days were simple—he worked, he read, he cooked, he tended his small garden. But more than anything, Thomás loved to build. His workshop was filled with unfinished projects—wooden chairs, delicate carvings, half-built instruments, and the frame of a door that had yet to find its home.

One evening, as he sat by the fire, there was a knock at his door.

A slow, deliberate knock.

Thomás hesitated. He wasn't expecting anyone.

He peeked through the window, but the porch was empty. Only the trees swayed in the night wind.

Cautiously, he opened the door.

A figure stood just beyond the threshold. Tall, hunched, wrapped in a tattered cloak that seemed to move on its own. The stranger's eyes were dark, unreadable, and when it exhaled, the air around it seemed to shudder.

"Let me in," the stranger said.

Thomás hesitated. Something about the voice pressed against his chest, like the weight of an unseen hand.

"No," he said, gripping the doorframe.

"Then I'll wait," the stranger whispered.

And it did.

The next morning, the figure was still there, crouched at the edge of the porch. It didn't knock this time—it only watched. The wind carried its breath through the house, making the walls creak.

Days passed. Then weeks. Thomás tried to ignore it, but the longer he did, the closer the stranger moved.

At first, it only sat by the steps. Then, it drifted to the window, its shadow stretching across the floor. Eventually, it slipped inside—not through the door, but through the spaces in between.

The hinges groaned under its weight. The air grew colder. The walls pressed inward.

And then, one day, Thomás stopped building.

He told himself he'd get back to it tomorrow. But tomorrow came, and the tools stayed untouched. The wood in his workshop gathered dust. The stranger had settled in now, lingering in the corners, growing taller, darker, heavier.

"There's no rush," it murmured. "What if it doesn't work out?"

"What if no one wants what you build?"

"What if you're not good enough?"

Thomás stayed in bed. He barely moved, barely ate. The house, once filled with the scent of sawdust and fresh earth, now smelled of emptiness.

Until, one morning, as light streamed through the window, he realized something:

The stranger had never forced its way in.

It had only ever waited to be let in.

And if it could enter through hesitation, through inaction—maybe it could leave through movement.

Slowly, Thomás sat up and swung his legs over the side of the bed.

The stranger only shivered.

Thomás stood and walked to his workshop.

The stranger loomed. It whispered. It tried to settle deeper into the space. But as Thomás reached for his tools, something happened.

With every cut of the wood, every turn of the chisel, the stranger shrank.

The weight in the house lifted. The air warmed. The walls expanded.

By the time the day was over, the builder stood before a finished door—the one he had abandoned weeks ago. And as he held it up to the light, he saw the stranger now no taller than a flickering shadow in the corner of the room.

"I will always be here," it murmured.

Thomás exhaled, wiping the dust from his hands.

"I know," he said.

"But you don't get to hold my hammer."

And with that, he picked up his tools and got back to work.

Contemplation

1. What fears in your life have you unknowingly made space for—through hesitation, doubt, or inaction?
2. What small action could you take today—no matter how imperfect—to reclaim your space and move forward, even with the presence of uncertainty?
3. If fear will always exist in some form, what would it look like to acknowledge its presence but not give it power?

Affirmation

I welcome the light of action into shadowed spaces.
Fear may visit, but it does not lead.
Each step I take reclaims my strength.
I move forward, even when doubt whispers.
My creative spark holds the hammer.

The Riverkeeper and the Well

There once was a man named Tomas, known as the Riverkeeper of his land. His village depended on the great river that flowed through the valley, providing water for crops, for animals, and for life itself.

For years, Tomas studied the river. He knew its currents, its seasons, its depths. He believed he understood its power—until one day, the river began to dry.

Panic spread through the village. Farmers feared for their fields. Merchants worried for their trade. Tomas journeyed upstream, searching for the cause.

What he found shook him to his core.

A neighboring kingdom had built a massive dam, diverting the river's flow for themselves. Their canals overflowed with water, while his own land turned to dust.

"They have stolen our lifeblood!" the villagers cried. "We must tear down the dam!" others shouted. Tomas's own heart burned with anger.

For the first time in his life, fear crept in.

Would the land wither? Would his people suffer? Was there any way forward if the river was gone?

And then—he stopped.

Fighting for what had already been taken would not bring the water back. Clinging to what was lost would only create more suffering.

He took a deep breath and remembered something he had always known but never fully understood:

Water does not belong to those who try to own it. It belongs to those who allow it to flow.

If the river could be stolen, then it was never truly infinite. If flow could be blocked, then it was never the true wellspring.

So instead of fighting, Tomas did something unexpected.

He walked into the hills, past the dying crops, past the empty wells. He climbed higher than anyone in the village had ever gone. And there, in the shadow of the great mountains, he listened.

He sat in stillness. He closed his eyes. He waited.

And then—he heard it.

A deep, quiet gurgling beneath the earth. A sound older than the river itself.

He began to dig.

At first, the villagers called him mad. "The river is gone, and you sit here, digging a hole?" But Tomas did not stop. He trusted what he had heard.

Insecurity whispered, "What if this well is not enough?"

Doubt warned, "What if the water does not come?"

But he did not cling. He did not force. He allowed.

And then, after days of silence—the water rose.

From deep within the earth, a fresh spring burst forth.

It was cleaner than the river had ever been. It belonged to no kingdom, no dam, no ruler. It had been there all along, waiting to be found.

Tomas smiled.

The river could be taken. The source never could.

And so, he did not hoard the water. He did not fear its loss. He let it flow.

And for as long as he remembered the true source of all things, his people would never thirst again.

Contemplation

1. When have you mistaken an external flow (money, ideas, success) for your true Source?
2. How do you react when you feel something has been taken from you?
3. When something important is taken from you, can you trust that something deeper is still available within you?

Affirmation

I listen for the spring beneath the silence.
The true Source cannot be blocked or stolen.
I am a vessel, not an owner.
What flows through me is alive, infinite, and free.
I trust the well that waits beneath all things.

THE WREN'S SONG

There once was a seeker of wisdom named Zariah who searched tirelessly for an answer to her universal question:

"Are we all One?"

She had studied sacred texts, traveled to distant lands, and sat at the feet of great spiritual teachers. Yet, no matter how much she learned, certainty always eluded her.

One morning, weary from her seeking, she decided to stop wandering. She sat by her window with her coffee, gazing outside but not really seeing. Light sparkled on the trees. Her thoughts drifted—questions, doubts, and plans tumbling over one another in her mind.

A bright, ringing call danced through the morning air—light and clear.

Shree! Shree! Shree!

A tiny wren, perched on a branch just beyond the glass, skipped from limb to limb, proclaiming its truth with fierce clarity.

Zariah froze. For a brief moment, the noise inside her head stopped. Her thoughts fell silent—not because she willed them to, but because the sound filled everything.

In that instant, she wasn't thinking. She wasn't searching.

She was simply listening.

A warmth spread through her chest, a subtle vibration down into her shoulders. Something ancient and true stirred within—not as a thought, but as a knowing.

The wren's song had done what no book, no journey, no teacher had ever been able to do.

It had returned her to presence.

And in that presence, she knew.

The answer wasn't earned. The truth of Oneness *was*.

She had only needed to stop and listen.

Contemplation

1. In moments of deep stillness, when thought falls away, do you experience separation—or do you sense that you have always been part of something greater?
2. Am you searching for answers outside of yourself that can only be felt within?
3. What sounds in your daily life could serve as portals to presence, if only you chose to truly listen?

Affirmation

I rest in presence and allow knowing to arise.
The truth of Oneness is not earned—it is remembered.
Each moment offers me a way home.
I listen, not with my mind, but with my being.
In stillness, I hear the song of Spirit.

Tacita and the Unshaken Tree

In a quiet village, there lived a woman named Tacita. She carried herself with grace, yet inside, she often felt conflicting emotions. One day, she found herself troubled—an elder of the village, a person she had once trusted, spoke words of kindness but acted differently.

Something within her ached. It echoed a feeling she had carried since childhood—a quiet ache, always beneath the surface.

How could someone's words be inconsistent with their actions?

Seeking solace, Tacita walked beyond the village to the great olive tree—its roots deep in the earth, its branches stretching toward the sky. She sat beneath its silvery leaves, closed her eyes, and called upon the voice within her—the voice that had always been there, waiting to be heard.

"Higher Self," she whispered, "what should I do?"

The wind moved through the leaves, as if whispering back.

"First, feel. Let yourself feel. Don't shrink from your emotions; they are not weakness. They are messengers, bearing your truth."

So Tacita did. She allowed the frustration, the sadness, and the anger to rise—to be acknowledged, to exist without apology. She did not run from them. She did not rush to silence them. She simply let them be.

Then, the voice spoke again.

"You are no longer that child. You are not in danger now. You can stand in who you are. You don't need to run—but you don't need to move before you're ready."

Tacita exhaled. For so long, she had learned to disappear, to make herself smaller when she felt unappreciated. But now, she realized—she did not need to shrink. She did not need to fight. She only needed to be.

She looked up at the ancient tree above her. Even the olive tree doesn't reach upward before settling deep into the earth.

And she understood. She did not need to know her next step today. She did not need to flee or to force a decision.

She only needed to root herself in her truth—to gather her strength, to settle into stillness.

"Then when will I know it is time to move?" she asked.

The voice within her smiled.

"You won't see the path until you're ready to walk it. But when the time comes, you will move—not from fear, but from truth."

Tacita leaned back against the trunk, feeling its silent wisdom.

She would not rush.

She would not run.

She would wait.

She would root.

And when the moment came, she would know.

Contemplation

1. Where in my life am I experiencing a disconnect between someone's words and actions—and how does that make me feel?
2. Am I seeking clarity or action too quickly, when I might first need to root myself in stillness and truth?
3. How can I remember that my value is not defined by others, but by my unshakable connection to Spirit?

Affirmation

I honor what I feel without apology.
I am rooted in truth, not fear.
I willingly pause before reacting.
Stillness is my strength.
When it is time, I will rise.

THE CHARIOTEER HAD A DREAM

Vigilus, the Charioteer, had a dream. Not a dream that fades with waking, but the kind that rises from within and takes root in the heart.

In this dream, he saw a valley of flowering trees—alive with color and stillness, a place where his Spirit could rest, and his heart could fully open. He didn't know where it was, only that it called to him with the voice of something remembered.

So he set out again, across the arid plain.

The sun was high, the land cracked and dry, but his four horses moved in rare harmony.

Mind no longer raced ahead.

Body moved with strength but without strain.

Emotion flowed without flooding.

And Ego, once proud and possessive, had softened into quiet watchfulness.

Vigilus held the reins gently now—like an artist holding a brush, like a prayer without words. He had practiced long for this: the art of allowing.

For hours, he traveled in silence, guided only by the inner pulse of his dream.

Then, as the horizon dipped, the path turned.

A sudden curve along a ridge.

On one side, a sheer drop.

On the other, a wall of stone.

There was no way to see what lay ahead.

And fear returned—not loud, but tight in the chest. What if the chariot slipped? What if the horses stumbled? What if the dream had led him wrong?

The horses sensed it.

Mind began to calculate.

Body stiffened.

Emotion stirred like a rising wind.

Ego leaned forward, urging control.

But Vigilus went inward.

"Spirit is in all things—the horses, the clouds, even this rocky road."

"And surely Spirit moves through me, as me."

"The path is solid."

"I am grateful for this adventure."

"I trust. I let go."

He breathed.

He held the vision, not the fear.

And as the chariot crested the curve—the road rose to meet the wheels.

What had seemed empty became solid.

What had looked like a drop became a bridge.

The path had always been there—waiting for his trust to reveal it.

He did not cheer.

He did not weep.

He simply smiled, and gave thanks.

From that day, Vigilus knew:

Spirit is not only the horses, the chariot, or the driver.

Spirit is the dust, the wind, the breath,

the desire, the dream, the unfolding.

It is the road beneath the wheels and the call of the horizon.

And all it ever asked of him was to hold the vision—and let the way appear.

Contemplation

1. What dream feels like a memory returning—something already yours, waiting to unfold?
2. When fear crosses your path, how can you return to trust, rather than control?
3. Can you see Spirit not only in beauty and ease, but also in the uncertain curve—the part of the road that tests your trust?

Affirmation

I ride the edge of the unknown with grace.
The path rises to meet my knowing.
I hold the vision gently—like a silent prayer.
Spirit moves in wind, stone, and breath.
Each step carries me home.

Gather Around the Parable

A guide for forming a spiritual discussion circle

When I first began this journey as a Spiritual Artist, I believed I was alone on my own path. It felt deeply personal—and for a while, it was. But over time, I've realized how critically important community is to spiritual growth. Perhaps challenging for my lone wolf self to understand, but we don't grow without the presence of others.

Social media has given us the illusion of connection—a kind of fast-food community that often leaves us with a deeper sense of separation and non-belonging. Now, more than ever, we must return to real connection. Face-to-face. Heart-to-heart.

Take the time to gather with others. Share ideas. Feelings. Time. Presence.

While this book can absolutely be used as a solo practice, it becomes even more powerful when shared. As a group, we create an amplified field of intention—a spiritual resonance that goes beyond what any one of us can hold alone. Consider forming a small group of friends, creatives, or seekers and meeting once a week to read and reflect on a single parable together.

You don't need a formal structure or deep theological training—just a willingness to listen, reflect, and be present.

How to Begin

- Invite 2 to 6 others who are open to spiritual exploration.
- Choose a regular meeting time—weekly, biweekly, or monthly.
- Begin each session by reading one parable aloud.
- Sit in a few moments of quiet before discussing.

Suggested Questions for Group Sharing

- What line or moment stood out most to you?
- How did this parable mirror something in your own life?

Gather Around the Parable

A guide for forming a spiritual discussion circle

When I first began this journey as a Spiritual Artist, I believed I was alone on my own path. It felt deeply personal—and for a while, it was. But over time, I've realized how critically important community is to spiritual growth. Perhaps challenging for my lone wolf self to understand, but we don't grow without the presence of others.

Social media has given us the illusion of connection—a kind of fast-food community that often leaves us with a deeper sense of separation and non-belonging. Now, more than ever, we must return to real connection. Face-to-face. Heart-to-heart.

Take the time to gather with others. Share ideas. Feelings. Time. Presence.

While this book can absolutely be used as a solo practice, it becomes even more powerful when shared. As a group, we create an amplified field of intention—a spiritual resonance that goes beyond what any one of us can hold alone. Consider forming a small group of friends, creatives, or seekers and meeting once a week to read and reflect on a single parable together.

You don't need a formal structure or deep theological training—just a willingness to listen, reflect, and be present.

How to Begin

- Invite 2 to 6 others who are open to spiritual exploration.
- Choose a regular meeting time—weekly, biweekly, or monthly.
- Begin each session by reading one parable aloud.
- Sit in a few moments of quiet before discussing.

Suggested Questions for Group Sharing

- What line or moment stood out most to you?
- How did this parable mirror something in your own life?

- What part of you resisted the message—and why?
- What deeper truth are you ready to accept or live out this week?

I've learned that when you feel resistance to a specific parable, that's a sign that there is an opportunity for the most personal growth. Take time with it. Let it sink in.

Let everyone share, without interruption or correction. Trust that something deeper begins to form—not just in the words, but in the silence, the shared presence, the spiritual coherence of the group. Let the wisdom rise from the space between you.

The power of parable lies in its simplicity—how it speaks to each of us differently, depending on where we are. When we gather around a story, we also gather around each other's hearts.

If this book has moved you, share it. Read it aloud. Listen deeply.

And trust that something sacred happens when we sit with truth . . . together.

To connect further

Explore more reflections, podcast episodes, and resources at:

www.spiritualartisttoday.com

The Spiritual Artist Podcast
(available on all major platforms)

The Spiritual Artist with CJMiller

Interested in going deeper?

Join me for a Spiritual Artist Retreat—a space to create, reflect, and reconnect with your Creative Intelligence. Retreat details and registration can be found on the website:

www.spiritualartisttoday.com

Find your Tribe.

Follow "The Spiritual Artist Podcast" on all major podcast directories or our YouTube channel.

Christopher J. Miller shares stories of enlightenment and growth with today's spiritual artists and thought leaders. Conversations explore how making art engages us in emotional, holistic, and spiritual development. Chris is an intentional artist available for online coaching and public speaking.

Available on Apple Podcasts, Spotify, Amazon Music, Pandora, and Google Podcasts.